America and the Limits of the
Politics of Selfishness

America and the Limits of the Politics of Selfishness

Sidney R. Waldman

LEXINGTON BOOKS

A division of
ROWMAN & LITTLEFIELD PUBLISHERS, INC.
Lanham • Boulder • New York • Toronto • Plymouth, UK

LEXINGTON BOOKS

A division of Rowman & Littlefield Publishers, Inc.
A wholly owned subsidary of The Rowman & Littlefield Publishing Group, Inc.
4501 Forbes Boulevard, Suite 200
Lanham, MD 20706

Estover Road
Plymouth PL6 7PY
United Kingdom

British Library Cataloguing in Publication Information Available

Library of Congress Cataloging-in-Publication Data

Waldman, Sidney R., 1940–
   America and the limits of the politics of selfishness / Sidney R. Waldman.
      p. cm.
   Includes bibliographical references and index.
   ISBN-13: 978-0-7391-1573-2 (cloth : alk. paper)
   ISBN-10: 0-7391-1573-1 (cloth : alk. paper)
   1. Political ethics—United States. 2. Representative government and
representation—United States. 3. United States—Politics and government—Moral
and ethical aspects. 4. Political leadership—United States. 5. Political science—
Philosophy. I. Title.

JK468.E7W35 2007
172—dc22   2006030816

Printed in the United States of America

∞™ The paper used in this publication meets the minimum requirements of
American National Standard for Information Sciences—Permanence of Paper
for Printed Library Materials, ANSI/NISO Z39.48-1992.

For Kay, Sophia, Erika, Lincoln, and the American people

Contents

~

Acknowledgments

I have spent more than four decades teaching Haverford and Bryn Mawr college students, often with great pleasure. Many of the ideas in this book emerged over the course of that teaching. I feel I have taught variations on one course, now in more than its fortieth year. I thank my students for participating with me on this journey, and I thank Haverford College for its continuing support. Both my teaching and this book taught me, and I am grateful for that. I also wish to thank my friends, Steve Boughn, a wonderful lunch companion, an astronomer, and a closet political analyst; the late Wilson Carey McWilliams, whose mastery and range never ceased to amaze me; and Ted Volckhausen who seems to know about everything. Andrew McFarland and Audrey Faulkner carefully reviewed this manuscript and made helpful suggestions, a few of which I followed. Carey McWilliams also read this manuscript and was encouraging. Richard Fenno has been encouraging and helpful throughout my career, and I am pleased to acknowledge him here. Harvey Glickman, Rob Mortimer, and Sara Shumer were fine colleagues for close to four decades. So too are my current colleagues, Steve McGovern, Susanna Wing, Craig Borowiak, Cristina Beltran, and Anita Isaacs. I also especially want to acknowledge some of my teachers, from high school through just a couple of years ago, Ted Repsholdt, Elizabeth Breden, Andrew Bongiorno, George Lanyi, Don Matthews, Robert Rupen, and, most recently, Carey McWilliams and Marcel Gutwirth. My son, David, has been a long-time intellectual partner. I pay tribute here to three other teachers of whom I am very proud, all members of my family, David, Laura, and Heather. I also wish to acknowledge my parents, Ben and Lillian, who lived some of the ideals presented in this book, each in their own way. It is with great pleasure that I dedicate this book to my three grandchildren, Sophia, Erika, and Lincoln, may they have a life as rich as mine; to America and the American people in whom I continue to have hope and faith; and to my wonderful partner, Kay Reed. There are none like her. Pro Gloria Dei.

CHAPTER ONE

~

Introduction

Many of the important analyses in this book, whether of Congress, the president, the public, or public policy, reveal the critical importance of morality. Is this new or surprising? Not if one goes back to political theory. What may be surprising is that careful empirical analysis reveals the importance of morality, whether it's in seeing the significance of congressional leeway and how it's used; understanding the limits of presidential leadership, including transformational leadership; and comprehending limits in our capacity to solve some of our most important problems.

Does this book tell us, or do we already know in practice, how to get people to be moral; that is, to act morally more consistently and frequently? Unfortunately not, though at the end of the book we will suggest some things that may be helpful. If this work is important, it is because it brings morality again to the center of politics and to the study of politics where it belongs.

I had no idea when I studied Congress, the presidency, and public policy that so many of the roads, after the most careful and deep analysis, would lead to morality, and the importance of choice. Perhaps the final destination was inevitable and obvious, especially in retrospect, but it is nonetheless of the highest importance.

How Is Our Political System Doing?

How does our political system stack up? How are we doing, and how shall we go about answering this question? What criteria shall we use? One good place to start is with the criteria of our Founders, in particular, the authors of *The Federalist Papers*. They understood that the purpose of government was the public interest and were not afraid to use that concept. They feared what could injure "the permanent and aggregate interests of the community."[1] They feared majorities, numerical minorities, and officeholders, each of whom could threaten the public good. They saw that human nature, above all what they referred to as self-love, which I will argue can easily lead to selfishness, produced factions that threatened individual rights and the public good. We need to take these ideas seriously and ask how our political system does when judged against these standards.

How have we done by these criteria? Do Congress and the president serve the public interest? To what extent? Within what limits? What threatens and injures the interests of our community? Do majorities, numerical minorities, and officeholders sometimes threaten the public good or not serve it? If so, can our political system deal with that and does it? How great a problem is selfishness for our democracy? In our examination of American politics we will attempt to grapple with these questions to see how we are doing. This is not merely of academic interest. The events of 9/11 showed us what people disaffected with us are capable of. Even were we not threatened by terrorists, however, what is at stake is important. The quality of our country is what is at stake. We begin with a preview of our argument.

The Argument

Puzzles of representation exist in American politics. Only about 10 percent of House districts are competitive, and research shows that most citizens do not hold their representatives responsible for the performance of Congress. This gives leeway to representatives, who are judged superficially in a variety of ways, for example, on the positions they take rather than on what they actually do and achieve. Because of the way they are judged, representatives are in a position that allows them not to consider the general interest. Their constituents find it hard to hold them accountable for what they do because the public often lacks the knowledge and the will to do so. On the other hand, the representatives' hypervigilance leads them to represent both general and particular interests more than one might expect in light of voter ignorance. Nevertheless, the lack of competition in most congressional districts, both because of the role of money in elections and because of the gerrymandering of congressional districts, is inconsistent with our emphasis on electoral competition and the competition of ideas. This lack of competition also contributes to voter ignorance in a self-reinforcing process.

Paradoxically, despite the citizens' low level of knowledge of their representatives, which could lead to an irresponsible Congress that sees little need to serve the public interest, Congress does try to serve the public interest, often on major issues facing the country, for example, in the areas of energy policy, macroeconomic policy, and social security. It can do so, even when actions in the public interest are unpopular, because representatives have developed ways of obscuring their action in order to give themselves political cover. Through these means, which we describe, representatives have leeway, room for choice, which they can use for good or ill. Representatives not only have leeway or freedom in the actions they take, but leeway in choosing the basis by which they decide what to do. Once the importance of this leeway is seen, we must ask what determines how it is used and see the profound implications of that for our political system. Basically politicians are in a position to choose the good. Once this is seen, we must ask how to get good people to run, what encourages and what discourages them, what determines who is successful and what role we as citizens have in that. We also must ask whether we will support our representatives, once elected, in their effort to do the good, and this raises important questions about us.

Legislative accountability, citizens' ability to hold their representatives accountable for their actions, clearly affects what kinds of representatives we will have. Unfortunately, with regard to Congress as a whole and the individual representative, this accountability is more difficult and more problematic than it seems. Nevertheless, analysis and experience show that the American people can hold Congress collectively responsible. To take one example, if one party has a ten-seat majority, even if only 10 percent of House districts are competitive, which has been the recent reality, and if both parties share those competitive seats equally, by winning slightly more than seven of every ten competitive seats the previous minority party can gain majority control of Congress, which can have a decisive effect on governing. By changing majority control of Congress, the American people can hold Congress collectively accountable. Because representatives are hypervigilant and sensitive to their electoral vulnerabilities as well as to possible ways to generate electoral support, both individually and as a party, they are more responsive to the people, including intense minorities, larger if less intense publics, and to moneyed interests. These different interests can push them in different directions.

Since the president and Congress sometimes do act in the public interest even when the action is not being called for by the people, and because they have the leeway to do so, it is important to elect good people to public office. Changes in campaign financing and in media coverage of politics and government might make it more likely good people would run and be elected. At the same time, citizens' selfishness keeps many of us out of public service.

If representatives and the leeway they have are important to our political system, to what extent do we also depend on the quality of leadership we have, not only in our legislative representatives, but in the president? To do their job, presidents rely on transformational as well as transactional politics, and the former almost always involves moral leadership, a leadership that tries to get us to see our own moral values and apply them to our social reality in order to change that reality.[2] However, because the president's moral appeals often fall on our deaf ears, his power to help us solve some of our major problems is often quite limited. In other words, we the people often ultimately determine whether our country will solve some of its most important problems. Leaders who would appeal to us must evoke unresolved problems that exist in our country and suggest ways to solve them consistent with and based on our beliefs and values. But if, because of self-love, we don't see or care about these problems, little can be done. The challenges our leaders and representatives present to us are often affected by our self-love. If our leaders do not believe we will respond to certain challenges because of our self-love, they are less likely to present them. This work focuses on the importance of and the problems caused by self-love, citizens' self-love, in political life. Self-love here means an exclusive or excessive regard for oneself and one's interests, including those of one's family, basically a self-concern unbalanced by a concern for others (beyond one's own family).

Leaders can attempt to teach deep moral truths, but will citizens be receptive to these truths and be prepared to support action on their behalf? Once again, the people's morality is critical in affecting what happens. Just as important, what and how we experience realities and whether we care about the reality and fate of others are absolutely critical in our reactions toward particular problems the country faces and what we are willing to support to deal with them. One can see this in the difference between what we were willing to support to deal with terrorist threats and our response to the problem of failing education in certain areas of our country, areas where we don't live. As a consequence, our leaders do not attempt certain things, for which we sometimes criticize them, but the fault and responsibility are ultimately ours. Our morality and what affects it are critical to politics.

Political leadership should be and often is moral agency. Without moral leadership the president cannot do what he needs to do and should do.[3] Bargaining alone cannot get the job done when it comes to certain matters. Once one sees the need for moral leadership, one realizes the need for cultural leadership. That leadership will utilize our emphasis on the market and economic individualism, but also emphasize democratic individualism to partly compensate for the inequality created by the market.[4]

Analysis shows how our legislative representatives have some leeway in acting, and thus we see the potential importance of morality in affecting how they use that leeway. We also will see how leadership, even transformational leadership, if it is to succeed, requires that we respond to moral appeals from the leader, and thus we see again the importance of morality in affecting what our country can achieve.

How else does the public affect what this country can achieve? Looking at education as a case study shows the role of the public in affecting what problems our government can solve. While failing education in our cities and rural areas limits the opportunity of those in the failing school systems, and hence limits the attainment of one of our core values, opportunity, the people of this country are not prepared to do what it would take to change this, which limits what our leaders and representatives can achieve. Because we blame our representatives and various others for the failure to fix the problem, we fail to see the critical role we play in the failure. If the people do not believe a particular problem can be fixed *or* do not care about that problem because it does not affect them or their family, as they see matters, then government's ability to fix the problem is limited. This can and does limit government in helping those who are weaker in the society.

The ability of our government to solve certain important problems in society is limited by the lack of support of our people, a lack largely due to our selfishness and self-love. Self-love affects our attitudes toward government and politics. The poor and the weak are limited in what they get politically and are vulnerable because of the place of self-love in our politics and society. The rich and middle class are in a better position to serve themselves governmentally than the poor. Because of our selfish concerns and our belief that most of what we want we will get from the private sector, most of us pay little attention to politics and government except as spectators. Because of superficial involvement in politics and our lack of knowledge of policy, we are probably more vulnerable to demagogic appeals in crises when we wish to take advantage of our democracy by changing leaders and policies. Equally important, if the majority does not care enough about certain critical problems faced by particular numerical minorities, most notably the poor, democracy is of limited utility to such minorities.

Because of our selfishness our country is likely to solve certain problems and unlikely or much less likely to solve others. For example, we are likely to find a way to deal with Social Security's and Medicare's fiscal problems, even if that involves accepting certain costs, because most people value, expect, and hope to benefit from these programs. We are likely to find ways to deal with budget deficits eventually because Wall Street and the business community are powerful, dislike deficit-driven interest rates, and their success affects the prosperity of most of us. In contrast, we are far less likely to solve the problem of failing education for the poor and all that contributes to it because most people do not care enough to demand a solution. This affects what kind of democracy we are. What problems we solve and which we fail to solve depends in large measure on our selfishness, a self-love that ignores the situation of others because of a too exclusive concern with oneself and one's family, and this self-love is tied to certain cultural beliefs we have, for example, individualism and self-reliance.

Many of the problems we face, if we are to resolve them, require our morality and compassion followed by action. This is true both for citizens and officeholders. That then raises the question of the role of religion since it can be a source of morality and compassion. However, religion, morality, and compassion, as they exist in most people now, will not solve the problems described in this book. Nevertheless, morality, compassion, and religion developed in us could be enormously helpful. Each of these faces challenges in helping us change our practice. Nevertheless, each is relevant and merits careful attention as part of the study of politics and society. Each deserves central attention if we are interested in solving our most important unresolved problems. Without morality and compassion we probably cannot resolve some of the most important problems our country faces, both domestically and in the world. In this work the focus is mostly on the problem of failed education since that so touches the heart of our core values, opportunity and freedom.

In assessing the role of the public in our political system one needs to recognize and then explain the public's skepticism and cynicism toward politics and identify their effects on our politics. These attitudes reduce our political involvement and participation, as do other factors, including the fact that the private sector and government do so much for us already, thus reducing our motivation to get politically involved. Because our involvement in politics is so limited and we are politically isolated from each other, we are more subject to demagogic manipulation and less able to control the influence of money over politics. Paradoxically, despite the limits in public participation and discourse in America, representatives can be held accountable, are held accountable on some important matters, and know it.

To evaluate our political system we need a concept of the public interest, which can help us decide what to focus on, what to study, and how to assess the nature and significance of what we find. We assume in our political arrangements that people think about and know their own interests, especially their self-interest, and sometimes we assume people will think about the public interest. It is not hard to show that people often not only do not know what is in their own self-interest, but often have a distorted view of the public interest. For example, our ability to recognize the public interest is limited because we don't see how our own material interests, let alone our human interests, are adversely affected by poverty and racism. We are often unable to experience and thus really know the costs suffered by others in situations very different from our own. As a consequence, we are incapable of knowing the public interest because our view is literally too limited, cognitively, analytically, and, most important, experientially. If we don't know our own interest or know only part of it and don't know the public interest or know only part of it, how do we function in a political system that is based on the notion that we will pursue our interests and our happiness? Because our conception of ourselves is limited, because we haven't fully realized who we are, our view of our happiness is also limited and even at least partly mistaken.

Because we do not fully understand our self-interest and the public interest, our freedom is less valuable, and we are less free. Of course, our freedom is real, but limited in ways we do not realize. Because we are not fully free, we do not see the limits of our freedom. If we are to deal with the problem of excessive self-love, which is intimately related to our partial blindness, morality and religion will have to play a role, even though they have often failed and been misused and abused in the past. Compassion and its absence also affect the moral limits of our political system, and it is also a subject that should be central to the study of politics.

The lack of discourse and reflection in the public, an absence reinforced by the commercial interests of television, is also a weakness in our political system. Because of this lack, including our not really listening to each other, we are not taking full advantage of the free speech we so value.

Morality also plays a role we rarely recognize in affecting whether we can provide ourselves, in our efforts at self-government, with what the economists refer to as "public goods," goods whose benefit we get whether we have contributed to their production or not. Often such goods are not attained because individuals lack sufficient incentive to contribute to their attainment, for example, they don't think their actions will make a difference. But if enough people are moral and get pleasure from acting morally, that selective benefit, the pleasure that goes with the action itself, can motivate enough people to act to produce the public good!

How shall we evaluate our political system? One way is to see if we can solve some of our most important problems, particularly those related to our core values. The failure of our educational system for the poor and disadvantaged, which affects their opportunities and freedom, is a stain upon our country and our political system. The American people have not supported and do not support what it would take to solve this problem, which suggests we do not hold the values we claim to hold, in particular opportunity, when it comes to certain others. The public suffers from a failure of compassion here, partly because of its inability to really see what is happening to certain others, and partly because it doesn't want to see. This failure of compassion in the public limits presidential and other political leadership.

One of the president's most important bases of leadership is cultural, his ability to draw on our core values. While economic individualism is often seen as our core value, self-love underlies that value and is at the heart of who we are. This self-love usually includes the desire to do well for our family as well as ourselves. Self-love in itself is not bad if it's not exclusive or excessive. However, it needs to be balanced by a focus on others, not just on one's own family. Both self-love and whether and how we can balance it greatly affect our collective self-government, the heart of our democracy. An understanding of our political system and how it serves and fails to serve opportunity and freedom shows we have more work to do to be true to our better selves and to what we say we stand for.

We face a severe problem of accountability in our democracy, a political system that places such weight on holding our leaders accountable. In this dangerous world, policies we adopt may lead to irreparable, irredeemable harm, and the leaders who made these policies, particularly the president, may no longer be in office when this harm occurs. To deal with this problem we citizens and our officeholders must do a better job anticipating the consequences of our government's actions. In these times it is very much in our interest to take on new responsibilities as citizens, to become better and more active electors and monitors of our government. A second way to deal with this problem of accountability is for Congress to have more power in the area of foreign policy and security as a check on the president. This is not without risk, but in light of the dangers involved in a world of terrorism and weapons of mass destruction, dangers that could be made more probable as a result of bad policy decisions, increasing Congress's influence in the area of foreign policy and security so it is a more equal partner with the president is probably desirable.

Just as we often ignore the needs of certain people in this country as we focus on our own needs and wants, we do the same regarding the rest of the world. The events of 9/11 showed us one result of that. Because of the development of weapons of mass destruction, which inevitably are spreading around the world, we are and will be vulnerable to attack as never before. While it is very much in our interest to reduce the motivation of others to do damage to us, we seem blind to its causes and the distresses of the world as we often are to the distresses of our country. Self-love, ignorance, and indifference have blinded us. What will it take for us to get beyond our excessive and exclusive self-love since doing that may be as essential to our interests as anything we do. There are alternative ways of doing this. We may be able to move beyond excessive self-love because it is in our self-interest to do so. Unfortunately it is often not clear to us that it is in our self-interest to do so. So counting on self-love to solve the problems created by excessive self-love may be a mistake. Compassion seems unable to help us avoid the immoral and possibly dire consequences of excessive self-love. Excessive self-love represents a failure of compassion or its too limited nature. The gap of distance, experience, and time between us and others and our self-love limit our compassion. While Madison argued that we cannot count on moral or religious motives to limit our self-love, the approaches of various religions to this problem are interesting and important.[5] Basically a number of religions teach that we know or have been taught what to do and that it is a matter of doing it. Many religions focus on compassion and the worst off of us.[6] Moses in his last sermon said we know what to do as did Buddha.[7] Even the general guidelines of different religions are similar; for example, Jesus, "Therefore, whatever you want men to do to you, do also to them," and Rabbi Hillel, "What is hateful to you, do not do to your neighbor."[8] Religions also know and teach that often we fail to do what we are supposed to do. Religious teaching, while often wise, seems not to be enough to get us to change our ways as we continue to ignore it or only follow it sometimes.

Philosophers have also turned to morality as they struggled with this problem, for example, Kant, Rousseau, Marx, Rawls, and numerous other philosophers. But that has worked no better than religion as a solution to this dilemma. In light of the limits of all these approaches in dealing with the problem of self-love, what shall we do? What is needed are the multiple fronts of self-love, compassion, religion, and morality with none of them either separately or together providing a panacea or guarantee we can solve the problem of excessive self-love. Compassion, morality, and religion can help us live better lives if only we will use them and pay loving attention to them as many of us pay attention to our children, our gardens, or whatever we love and care about. Because of their great effect on politics and thus their centrality in it, compassion, morality, and religion are a proper, important, and critical part of the study of politics.

What if we cannot deal with the problems caused by excessive self-love? Such self-love has produced bitter fruits, suffering, and destruction as well as positive achievements. But there are new, potentially devastating, realities in our time, and what we do in the coming years may affect whether and to what extent we suffer the consequences of our excessive self-love. One consequence, if we don't rectify this problem, will be a continuation of an unacceptable and unsustainable degree of inequality in our country and the world. It is very likely the inequality will become even greater than it is now. If no other consequence occurred, this would be bad enough and should be a source of shame. But more is at stake than this. The world is changing, and it is unlikely we can go on as we have been. The development of technology and the inevitable spread of weapons of mass destruction means that sooner or later terrorists are likely to get these weapons and use them against the more prosperous and powerful parts of the world, most likely with a special focus on us as the most powerful and rich country in the world. While we can fight a war against terrorism, it is unlikely we can stop all the efforts against us. It is also likely our war on terrorism will create new cadres of terrorists out for revenge. What we can and must do is seek to change the circumstances that produce terrorists, and that includes reducing inequalities in the world. The goal is not to eliminate inequality for that is not likely to happen and is not desirable, but rather to help people gain the basic necessities of life, including increasing their opportunity to gain these through productive labor. People want to believe that they and their children are moving in the right direction materially, that things will be better for their children. We can help them do this. It will not be easy and will require much more of a commitment than we have made so far. Nevertheless the obstacles to our achieving this are not greater than others we have overcome.

It is absolutely in our moral *and* material interest to deal with the problems caused by excessive self-love. If we do not, our futures are likely to be bleak. Of course, excessive self-love is not our only problem. We must also deal with our arrogance, our self-righteousness, and our desire to control the world in ways that cause great and widespread alienation and reaction. We need to recognize that helping those less well off do better will not entirely eliminate those who wish to do us evil, which is why there will always be a role for force, even as our *principal* thrust should be generosity. While we should do this for moral reasons, the practical reasons for doing so, based on our self-interest, are just as relevant and will probably be why we choose this path if we do. Will we have the wisdom and intelligence to see this or will we remain blind to our own interests and responsibilities? We cannot control the world, but we can help make it a more hospitable place for us and others.

There is an even more fundamental reason why we should deal with the excesses of our self-love. That is our job, our task here on Earth, not just for what it produces in the lives of others but also for what it means in our own lives. By dealing with excessive self-love, we will change our self and make it more worthy of the love of others, of our self, and of our Creator. We are all given choices in life, some of us have fewer constraints and more opportunities, some of us more constraints and fewer opportunities, but we all have choices in how we live, how we are with ourselves and others. Our task in life is to figure out what we are supposed to do and then do it, in practical and effective ways. This is a lifetime task, one worthy of us and of the blessings of life we have received.

What is at stake in all this is the quality of our country and the quality of our lives. Before these questions can be addressed, some puzzles of representative government in our country need to be examined.

Notes

1. Alexander Hamilton, James Madison, and John Jay, *The Federalist Papers* (New York: New American Library, 1961), 78.

2. Erwin C. Hargrove, *The President as Leader* (Lawrence: University Press of Kansas, 1998), 44.

3. James MacGregor Burns, *Leadership* (New York: Harper & Row, 1975), 3–4, 389.

4. Hargrove, *The President*, 52.

5. Hamilton, Madison, and Jay, *Federalist Papers*, 81.

6. Karen Armstrong, *The Spiral Staircase* (New York: Knopf, 2004), 293.

7. Karen Armstrong, *Buddha* (New York: Penguin, 2001), 148–49. Deuteronomy 13:11–14. In quoting the Bible, I have used the New King James Version.

8. Babylonian Talmud, Shabbat 31a.

CHAPTER TWO

~

Puzzles of Representative Government

Introduction

In this chapter we will see that representatives have leeway, room for freedom of action and thus choice, in what they do because voters know so little both about Congress and about their representatives. In light of voter ignorance, representatives could be irresponsible in their actions, but in a number of ways they are not. A close analysis of the actions of members of Congress shows their leeway in not only deciding what they will do but on what basis they will decide that. That leeway points us to the importance of their morality in affecting how they use it, which then raises questions about who runs for Congress, what affects that, and what affects who is elected. The argument then focuses on the importance of holding Congress collectively responsible and the problems faced in achieving that. The chapter ends with a discussion of how to get good people to run for public office. The most important point in this chapter is the leeway representatives have in what they do, which focuses our attention on their morality, which affects how they use it. As we will see in the rest of the book, morality, in particular our morality, will also be crucial in the public response to efforts of presidential leadership and to the role the American public plays in our politics, which ultimately affects the quality of our society.

The Puzzles of Representative Government

While we elect representatives in our republican government, we are so used to this system that we often fail to see the puzzles our system creates. These pose dilemmas that affect how our government works and whether it does the job it is supposed to. To begin with, Congress has 535 members in its two houses combined. In any election year each of us votes for at most two congressional representatives, one in each house. How can a citizen or, for that matter, the American people hold Congress as a whole responsible when each voter is only voting for one or two representatives, a representative and a senator. One can hold the president responsible by voting for or against him or his party at the next election. If you knew the majority party that controlled Congress and the White House, assuming one party controlled both legislative houses and the presidency, and didn't like what the government had done or were dissatisfied with the state of the country and blamed the government, you could vote against that party's candidate in a House and/or Senate election, but that is not what most American voters do. If they like their incumbent, and the evidence is that most do, often based on very little information, they will vote for him. Only about 10 percent of House districts are competitive. Over 90 percent of House incumbents who seek reelection are successful, and recently the Senate incumbent success rate has been about the same. We know that often most Americans have serious reservations about the job Congress is doing and also have reservations about the government as a whole, yet despite this the number of congressional incumbents voted out is very small. This suggests that citizens are not holding their representatives responsible for the performance of Congress. That leaves us with another puzzle. Can the people hold Congress collectively responsible and, if so, how?

Before answering that question, let us look at the behavior of our representatives to see what it tells us about our representative government. We know that members wish to be reelected so they engage in position-taking, symbolic politics, the provision of particularized benefits, and blame avoidance.[1] They are most frequently rewarded for the positions they take rather than what they achieve. In engaging in symbolic politics they often express an attitude rather than prescribing policy effects and often do not work hard enough through legislation and oversight to achieve the policy effects they say they desire. They provide particular benefits to specific individuals, groups, or constituencies in a way that allows them to claim credit for this. We also know that members are generally not rewarded by voters for legislative craftsmanship or for mobilizing their fellow members, two of the most important things representatives can do. It is doubtful most voters think about these aspects of a representative's behavior. When we add all this up, we see that representatives may not be doing their job and may also be taking a parochial point of view without considering the general interest. Further, they may be obscuring some of their actions and making it harder for the citizens to hold them accountable.[2] If they have the capacity and an incentive to do all this, we might ask whether the political system works well enough to do what it's supposed to do and, if so, how this occurs.

Before we attempt to answer that question, we might ask why representatives can successfully utilize position taking. It is because the people do not know what Congress has done. This occurs for a variety of reasons, including the complex nature of Congress. Action takes place in two houses and within each house, in subcommittees, committees, on the floor, and finally in conference committee where the effort is made to reconcile differing House and Senate versions of a bill. Therefore, keeping track of what is happening with particular legislation is difficult, even if citizens wanted to, which they generally don't. Often even with simple legislation, a bill can have multiple important parts and it is hard to keep track of it. In contrast to the complexity of Congress, the president is more readily readable. He can take a stand, repeat it endlessly, which often happens, and get repeated coverage so people are more likely to know what he stands for. By way of contrast, who speaks for Congress? Neither the Speaker of the House nor the Majority Leader of the Senate commands the stage as the president does. Congress speaks through its action, but its action on a piece of legislation changes through the legislative process, is hard to keep track of, and often gets little publicity. Even if you knew what Congress finally did or did not do, since there are 535 members, how would you know the role your representative or senators played? They don't get the coverage the president gets, in fact generally they get very little coverage.

How then shall a citizen hold his representative accountable? One could look at his votes, including on amendments to bills, but few avail themselves of that opportunity, and understanding the significance of what is found often is not easy, especially if the purpose is to go beyond knowing the symbolic significance of the vote. The reality of Congress does not make it easy to hold representatives accountable unless some reasonable and practical way to do so can be found.

As pointed out, members take positions and are rewarded for these, not for legislation passed and whether it will achieve its purposes. Less frequently realized, this is also true when representatives are judged by how they vote. Thus, citizens usually cannot distinguish what legislation is supposed to achieve from what it actually achieves and thus cannot distinguish symbolic action from action that will make a difference. There are a number of reasons for this. First of all, voters usually don't know what legislation has passed, let alone what it includes, even generally. For example, two-thirds of the people in July, 1993, did not know deficit reduction was part of President Bill Clinton's economic plan even though that was the first and major item of Clinton's presidency and took up much of the politics of his first year.[3]

Because citizens don't know what role their own representative has played in the passage of legislation—at most they'll very occasionally know his floor vote—the representative cannot easily get credit for his specific action in dealing with national problems. Usually the most he can say is he voted for the prescription drug benefit in Medicare or that he is for it. On rare occasions, as a committee or subcommittee chair or as one of the top party leaders, he may get credit or blame for his leading role on controversial and important legislation. Thus the representative seeks particularized benefits for specific constituencies because he can claim and get credit for getting them enacted.[4]

The reality of our democracy is limited in other ways. Voters know very little about how their representative has voted, even generally. Only about half the voters can say whether they generally agree or disagree, or agree and disagree about equally, with their incumbent's votes.[5] Only 18 percent could say they agreed or disagreed with their incumbent's vote on a particular bill, any bill.[6] If half the voters do not know about their incumbent's votes generally and four-fifths do not know about any specific vote the incumbent cast, how do they evaluate their representative?

The basis of voter approval of representatives is superficial. If voters recall the name of their representative or even can, when his name is listed for them, rate him on a scale of 0 to 100 (50 being neutral), they are more likely to like and vote for the candidate.[7] Why remembering the name or even being able to rate it (and most ratings are positive at about 60) should lead to liking is not clear. If liking the incumbent leads to name recall and familiarity, what causes the liking? Exposure in the media, whether through television, radio, or newspaper, affects familiarity and liking, as does the amount of money the candidate spent. Recognizing the incumbent's name or being able to rate him on a scale certainly is not a demanding requirement. If it is familiarity that produces liking and a positive rating, we still have to ask why voters like their incumbent. Is it because they haven't heard anything bad about him and because they want to assume he is representing them unless they hear otherwise? If voters haven't heard anything bad about their representative, it may be because he hasn't done anything so egregious as to get their negative attention. Whatever the causes of this liking of the incumbent, it exists even when voters don't approve of Congress as a whole.

The desire to believe your leaders and representatives are taking care of you has been described as an escape from freedom.[8] After all, if someone is taking care of you in certain areas, you do not have to worry about taking care of yourself in those areas. Do voters need to believe their own representatives are representing their interests because they do not feel Congress or the government as a whole is doing that? Americans are curiously ambivalent about their government and their representatives. On the one hand, they want to believe their leaders will take care of them and represent their interests, note for example the attitudes toward a president just after he has been first elected and very early in his term. On the other hand, often attitudes toward the president and his administration change over time. Is this escape from freedom, a desire to believe your leaders and representatives are taking care of your interests, tied up with another escape, one from responsibility? If things go wrong in the public sector or the society or economy, it's the president's fault, the government's fault, Congress's fault. Somehow one's own congressional representative, whether in the House or Senate, is the last to be blamed, after the president and the Congress as a whole. One can see this in high incumbency success rates even when times and the economy are bad. For example, in 1980 and 1982 when the economy was bad, over 90 percent of House incumbents seeking reelection were successful.

One reason incumbents do as well as they do is because their constituents' knowledge of them is pretty limited. The person most likely to reveal the incumbent's shortcomings is his challenger, but very often the challenger is even less known than the incumbent.[9] Even when soft money could be donated to the national parties, most challengers weren't known and most races were not competitive.

Understanding the role of money in our electoral system helps explain the lack of competitiveness in most congressional districts. The amount of money spent in a campaign clearly affects electoral success and thus who is elected and who is represented. Money is particularly important for challengers because the more they spend, the better they do. To have a reasonable chance of winning, say a 35 percent chance, challengers need to spend $800,000 to $900,000 (in 1998 dollars). Only 2 percent of them, adjusting for inflation in the period 1972 to 1998, actually spent that much.[10] This is important in affecting our democracy. If most challengers cannot raise the money to be competitive and if they are the ones most likely to raise questions about the job incumbents are doing but do not have enough money to get on the radar screen, how limited are we in our choice of representative?

*We properly emphasize electoral competition and the competition of ideas as criti-
cal to our democracy, but in most congressional districts that competition hardly
exists.*

One reason so few challengers receive the money they need to make a real
race of it is because most have little chance of winning and thus contributors
see them as a bad investment.[11] Challengers have little chance of winning
because so many congressional districts are gerrymandered, created by state
legislatures to favor the party that controls these legislatures. Gerrymandering and the distribution of money may be the strongest forces limiting competition in elections for our representatives.[12] The limited competition that
results means that voters do not hear the challenger's criticisms of the incumbent, and thus they are less able to evaluate the incumbent.

It is a very important fact in American politics that most House districts
are not competitive in the sense that the election outcome could go either
way. While more Senate seats are competitive, the Senate incumbent success
rate is almost as high as the House rate. In other words, most congressional
races are not competitive. What is the significance of this for our democracy?
The answer is not as straightforward as it might first seem.

Even if only a tenth of House seats are competitive, and the representatives are hypervigilant and even paranoid about how they might be criticized
and believe they could be vulnerable, they will go out of their way to bolster
their support. This extra effort makes them not only better representatives of
their supporters and potential supporters insofar as they do what these people want and what they think will please them, but also makes representatives more supportive of certain money interests, which may or may not co-
incide with the interests of a majority of their constituents but which is
helpful in their reelection bids. There is some evidence of hypervigilance and
paranoia in certain cases—the tax reform act of 1986 is an example, but that
case was unusual because of the spotlight on it.[13] It is worth pointing out that
a certain amount of paranoia and hypervigilance in our representatives likely
facilitates our republican system. Because of it, our legislators better represent
their constituents than one might conclude from survey data of the sort we
have been looking at. Of course, representation can involve acting as a del-
egate, that is, doing what one's constituents want, or as a trustee, doing what
one decides is in the best interest of one's constituents. It is likely representatives' vigilance not only makes them better delegates in representing certain points of view, both those generally held and those held by particular
groups, but also makes them more likely to care about the welfare of the
country as it is generally evaluated by most of their constituents, for example
in the area of the economy, security, and on any other matters of concern to

a majority of their constituents. That Congress focuses on the economy and supports efforts to enhance security reflects this general concern, and the fact that it passes lots of legislation that favors numerically large interests as well as small ones, such as Social Security, Medicare, tax breaks for particular groups, and other programs, including progressive ones for numerically small interests, reflects this desire to represent many interests. *Thus Congress represents both general and particular interests more than one might expect in light of the limited voter knowledge surveys reveal,* and this contributes to the success of congressional incumbents.

What are other consequences when only a small minority of House districts are competitive? Because most districts are not competitive, there is little electoral incentive for their representatives to seek the middle ground. They don't need to appeal to a swing vote, which makes them more partisan and makes it harder to achieve bipartisan agreement in Congress. If there is any competition in these uncompetitive districts, it comes in the party primary with the primary challenger usually adopting a more extreme position. This pushes Republican incumbents to the right and Democrats to the left, again making it harder to achieve bipartisan agreement and creating a more partisan Congress.[14] A more partisan Congress is not necessarily a bad thing. This depends on your view of partisanship, but sometimes circumstances require bipartisanship, for example, when Congress needs to pass legislation that may be difficult, such as measures to enhance the finances of Social Security and Medicare or to reduce the deficit. In those instances a bipartisan Congress allows the parties to share responsibility in making difficult decisions. The deficit reduction that George H.W. Bush and the Democratic Congress achieved in 1990 was an example.

How can we make congressional districts more electorally competitive? One way would be to provide public financing of congressional campaigns. America has had public financing of presidential campaigns since 1974, but not of congressional campaigns. One problem, of course, is that Congress would have to pass this, and why would they pass legislation that makes it more likely they would face strong and strongly financed competitors, especially when there is no serious and sustained public pressure to do this? When this issue comes up, representatives often say, "I don't think taxpayer money should pay for the campaigns of politicians like me." The American people have responded positively to such statements. What the public fails to understand is that the current system of private contributions costs them when tax breaks or other subsidies are passed as a result of the influence of moneyed interests. Contributors make contributions to gain access, which they value because it leads to legislative influence, and much of the legislation it leads to costs citizens. That the public fails to take this into account in not pushing for public financing reflects their failure to understand what is going on. While most citizens understand the influence money has in politics and government, they don't see that in not paying for politicians in one way, they pay in another way and much more so.

The American system is filled with paradoxes and ironies. When one sees how little most citizens know about their representatives, one might expect an irresponsible Congress that sees little need to serve the public interest. Nevertheless, it is striking that often on major issues facing the country, probably more than one would expect, Congress does try to serve the public interest. Whether it is in energy pricing policy, macroeconomic policy, or so-cial security, to name a few areas, Congress has often passed legislation in the public interest. For example, in the late 1970s and 1980s Congress deregu-lated the price of oil and natural gas so that their prices would go up, not a popular result, in order to reduce consumption and increase domestic pro-duction. In 1990, 1993, and 1997 Congress passed deficit reduction bills that finally eliminated the deficit and produced a surplus even though that in-volved increases in taxes and cuts in spending, which were unpopular. In 1983 Congress found a way to put Social Security back on a financially sound footing for decades by raising the age when Social Security kicks in and in-creasing the payroll tax, both of which were not popular. In each of these cases Congress did what was arguably in the public interest.

Some of these areas where Congress acted in the public interest are also areas of interest to the business community and Wall Street where the lat-ter's interest coincided with the public interest. Congress reduced the deficit and deregulated the price of energy, both actions in the interest of the busi-ness community and arguably the public. In other areas, such as creating a sound fiscal basis for Social Security in 1983, the public interest was the in-terest of a very large number of people. But even in areas where Wall Street's and the business community's interest is peripheral and where the majority in this country doesn't care that much, such as education for the poor, Con-gress has sought the public interest to some extent and tried to figure out how to obtain it. One sees this in federal programs that aid poor schools, which have existed since the 1960s, although the limitations in the resources de-voted to those programs and what those programs have achieved also show the limited motivation behind such a commitment. If Congress and the American public cared more about education for the poor, they would not have tolerated the limited success of educational policy for so long. The fact that education policy for our poor schools has not been successful suggests that the American people have not demanded success. If this were the education of their own children, they would not tolerate this failure and they would have the numbers to back up their decision.

What allows Congress to act in the public interest even when doing so requires measures that might not be popular, for example, increasing the cost of energy in order to increase production and reduce consumption? *Congress can set things up to give representatives leeway in acting by obscuring their action and making it hard to trace so that explanations will not be required of them and, if required, will be accepted.* This leeway is extremely important in our political system in ways we will examine, but first we will look at examples of how it is achieved.

To take one example, representatives can pass legislation committing them to certain actions without specifying those actions, thereby postponing the tough decisions. They did this in passing spending limits in defense, domestic discretionary spending, and foreign aid in the deficit reduction bill of 1990.[15] Congress can also obscure the costs they impose on people as they did in the 1990 deficit reduction bill when they phased out personal exemptions and limited deductions for people whose adjusted gross income was over $100,000 a year. In passing that legislation they said they were raising the marginal tax rate on the wealthiest individuals from 28 percent to 31 percent, but in fact the real marginal tax rate was as high as 34 percent though they tried to obscure this through complicated tax code regulations. Congress can also provide itself leeway by imposing indirect rather than direct costs as they did in the 1990 Medicare spending cuts. Three-fourths of the Medicare savings were realized through lower payments to healthcare providers. Because these providers would get less from Medicare, they would try to pass their costs on to others, for example by charging more to non-Medicare patients. "These indirect costs were less likely to be noticed and less likely to be attributed to the actions of Congress and the votes of one's representative."[16]

Representatives can also insulate themselves, while doing politically difficult tasks, through bipartisanship. They did this in the 1990 deficit reduction bill when each party agreed to deliver at least half of its members plus one in the floor vote on the package and monitored that during House voting. Since the two parties worked together to pass deficit reduction, whom were the voters to blame? Congress also gives itself leeway when it authorizes someone else to act for it, as representatives did in 1975 when they delegated authority to the president to deregulate the price of oil as early as June, 1979. In doing this in 1975 representatives could get through the elections of 1976 and 1978 before oil prices went sharply up again, and two-thirds of the Senate would have faced reelection before the price increase. Thus, representatives

gave themselves some leeway by postponing the effect of their legislative action. Congress can also use its procedures to give its representatives leeway.
For example, when Congress decontrolled the price of natural gas in 1978,
raising its price to consumers, the House never voted on that pricing as a sep-
arate matter. Rather, representatives voted on it only as part of a huge natural energy plan containing many items. No critic of a representative could
point to a specific vote on natural gas decontrol that passed the House. A
representative could say she opposed natural gas decontrol but voted for the
national energy plan because on balance it was a good bill and did many good
things even though gas decontrol was a mistake. Where policy changes cannot be traced back to specific actions, representatives are less vulnerable to
attack. This nontraceability helps insulate members in their future elections,
and makes it less likely they will have to explain their actions.[17]

    *That representatives have ways to protect themselves when doing the unpopular
suggests a certain leeway or freedom they have in acting.* This is critically important. Once we realize the leeway they can obtain for themselves by doing
things in particular ways, we are led to ask why they do what they do, that
is, why they use their leeway as they do, which raises the question whether
we can know their motives. An example will help us see what is possible in
the analysis of motives and what of importance is revealed in attempting it.
The example we will use is the key congressional vote when President Reagan attempted to stimulate the economy and reduce the size of government
by cutting governmental spending and taxes in 1981.[18] This effort by Reagan
was extraordinarily important as it created large deficits that put permanent
constraints on government spending throughout the 1980s and into the
1990s. The key vote in the House on reducing spending was on a rule that
allowed for a single vote on Reagan's entire economic package. Under House
procedures the rule determines which amendments, if any, are in order in
voting on a bill. The rule must first be passed by the House before a bill can
be considered on the floor. The rule allowing for just a single vote on Reagan's bill passed, 216 to 212, and defeated another rule that would have divided the bill into six parts forcing representatives to vote to cut (1) Social
Security and public assistance (a popular and unpopular program combined,
not an accidental combination), (2) school lunches and student loans (a
program that served poor students and one that served mainly middle-class
students), (3) energy and commerce programs, (4) food stamps (a program
that served poor people, but also helped farmers), (5) subsidized housing, and
(6) cost-of-living adjustments for federal employees' salaries and pensions (a
program that mainly benefited middle- and upper-middle-class people). Key
people on both sides agreed that under the latter rule the president's program

would not have been approved.[19] What is interesting is that any member of Congress could have explained his vote on the rule, however he voted. Understanding that is critical to seeing the leeway representatives had. For example, a member could say, "I voted to consider the bill as a whole, not in parts, because it made sense as a whole package and needed to be considered that way." Or, if a representative voted against the rule treating the bill as one package, he could say, "Voters needed to understand what was in that package, what we were doing, and separating the bill into six parts revealed that. Besides, I favored some parts of the bill, not other parts, as I think my constituents do, and in a democracy we should be able to vote for what we're for and against what we're against and not be allowed to hide the bad with the good."

It is practically certain voters did not know the vote on the rule was the key vote on Reagan's program. It is also very likely they would have had much difficulty evaluating the above explanations had such explanations been requested, which was very unlikely. As we have seen, congressmen act in a variety of ways so that explanations will not be requested of them and, if requested, will be accepted.[20]

Clearly if a congressional district was pro-Reagan, its representative likely would have voted to support the president on this key, if obscure vote, and the majority of citizens would have approved had they known of the action and understood its significance. Similarly, a district opposed to Reagan and what he was trying to do would probably have a representative who voted against Reagan's program and for the rule that made its passage unlikely. This illustrates the importance of party and ideology in creating a connection between the representative and his constituents. But in closely divided districts representatives had leeway in how they voted, leeway enhanced by making the key vote an obscure procedural vote whose significance was not transparent to the ordinary citizen.

Thus the key vote on Reagan's economic policy in 1981 was on the House rule that made the vote on his many spending cuts (in 750 programs) a single vote, up or down, on the whole package rather than six votes on his program divided up as described above. It has been argued that the Reagan administration worked to make this procedural vote a key test of whether a legislator supported the president's program. "The administration transformed what was usually an obscure procedural matter into a very visible vote on the president's program, thus guaranteeing that future challengers could use this vote as if it were really a substantive vote on explicit economic policy."[21] From everything we know about our representative process it is practically inconceivable most voters knew about this procedural vote at the time

or even later under the prodding of a challenger. Remember that most challengers are not visible. Of course, a challenger in a primary or general election could claim the representative voted against or did not support President Reagan's spending cuts without going into detail. The incumbent could
choose to ignore the charge, not respond to it so as not to give the issue additional publicity. How much money would it take to repeat the charge often
enough to make it credible and make a significant electoral difference and
how many challengers have that amount of money? If attacked in this way,
the incumbent could give instances where he supported Reagan, and incumbents in swing districts probably would have given Reagan some support just
to be able to do that, even if they didn't support him on the spending cuts.
It is far from clear that elections in swing districts would turn on the incumbent's support for Reagan's spending cuts. Thus representatives from the key
swing districts had more leeway in casting a vote on the rule than Arnold
suggests.

Arnold makes a more important and valid point when he says "some legislators wanted to approve the president's program but could not do so without the protection of a closed rule."[22] He is describing how some representatives saw their situation. What Arnold does not examine, and this is critical,
is why some wanted to approve the president's program. There are a variety
of possible answers. Some might have wanted to give his program a chance
to work. Some members of his own party wanted to avoid embarrassing or
weakening the president. At least equally important, some may well have
thought the program of spending cuts would improve the economy when
combined with tax cuts (politically, to cut taxes you first had to cut spending) and that it was in the public interest to make these cuts. Another reason why some voted for these cuts is that they mainly fell on the working
poor, for example, the cuts in food stamps, public assistance, subsidized housing, and Medicaid, and many members did not have that many working poor
who voted in their districts so this was a politically easy way to go. Another
reason for voting for the program was that members wanted to look like they
were doing something about the economy and to also convince themselves
they were doing something. Similarly others voted against the program because they thought it was not in the public interest or to embarrass Reagan
and the Republicans, to mention two of several possible motivations.

There is no way to assess which of these motives were most influential.
*What the analysis shows is both the representatives' leeway in the action they took
and their leeway in deciding on what basis they would choose what to do.* A sufficient number of members had this leeway, and they determined the outcome.
This leeway can also be seen in the bidding war that went on between the

two parties as they cast about for votes on both the spending bill and later the tax bill.[23]

What was the possible effect of this bill on the economy and how did that affect representatives' decisions how to vote? If the economy recovered, for whatever reason, most incumbents would do well though the president's party in congressional elections would probably do slightly better.[24] If the economy remained in bad shape, whatever the reason, the president's party in Congress would be hurt more. That meant Republicans who thought the program really would improve the economy had a political as well as a public interest reason for supporting it. On the other hand, the electoral fates of most members would not turn on economic recovery since most incumbents are reelected even when the economy is not good. Of course, if representatives were paranoid about what could and might happen, they might vote based on their fears. They might also be concerned about how the economic cycle would affect the chances their party could maintain or gain control in Congress. Thus representatives might be concerned with the effects on the economy of the congressional votes on the tax and spending bills, which could make them vote for what they thought was the public interest, an improved economy. They also could have voted on ideological grounds, for example, to reduce the size of government, or to gain support from those who would benefit from a tax cut or to avoid the loss of support because of spending cuts. This again shows their leeway in deciding how to vote.

The likelihood citizens at the next election would connect the state of the economy with their legislator's vote on the president's program was very small. This gave representatives some leeway. If Democrats voted against the program and it failed to pass and the economy continued in the doldrums, Democrats were not likely to be hurt. Only in a district where most people agreed with Reagan and wanted to give his program a chance, for example, in Republican districts and in some districts in the South, might a Democrat in that context be in trouble if he voted the wrong way. In fact, it was incumbents in Republican districts and some southern Democratic incumbents from the South who voted for the Reagan program and passed it.

In his analysis of votes on the Reagan budget in 1981, Doug Arnold cites a senior Democrat who voted for the Reagan budget. "I don't see how this can hurt me. If it doesn't work, I'll run against it. And if it does work, nobody's going to be mad at me."[25] What Arnold does not say is that the same representative could have voted against the Reagan budget and said the same words! This shows the explanatory and voting leeway certain representatives had in these key votes. Of course, representatives from districts filled mostly with Reagan supporters as well as those from anti-Reagan districts did not have the same voting leeway except at their own peril. The swing vote in the House that ultimately determined Reagan's success was composed of representatives who could have voted either way. They were swing voters partly because they could have voted either way and survived.

The leeway we have identified in this case, and such leeway is not unusual, is extremely important because it leads us to ask what determines how the leeway will be used and then to see the profound implications of that for our political system. Once we recognize the leeway members have in voting, even on as important a matter as the Reagan budget in 1981, which set the tone for a good part of the next two decades, we see the room for choice representatives have in deciding what to do and in deciding what they will consider, think about, and how they will weigh these matters in making their choices. This shows the importance of and the need to elect good people, who will make good and thoughtful choices, and that does not necessarily mean electing someone who happens to agree with us. We have identified multiple possible reasons for deciding how to vote in this case. We want representatives who thoughtfully choose their reasons. We do not want someone who simply sells his vote to the highest bidder, for example, the one who gives him a large campaign contribution. While most citizens appreciate the need to elect good people, most do not understand the leeway representatives have and what allows and even necessitates it. This leeway is not itself problematic and is desirable and necessary, but everything turns on how it is used.

It is not surprising that the quality of our representatives and leaders, and of us, affects the quality of what they and we do, but it is important to see exactly how this plays itself out in specific cases and instances, which is the focus of this work. *It is too easy to see politics as inevitably election and money driven with no room for choice, to see politicians as people trapped by their profession and unable to choose the good. Once the room for choice is seen, that inevitably raises questions about how we get good people to run, what encourages and what discourages them, and also raises questions about how we elect our representatives, that is, what determines who is successful and what role we as citizens have in that.* Clearly the role of money in elections is relevant here as is the ignorance of the typical voter. How much better off we would be with the public financing of congressional campaigns and how much better we citizens can do in ordinary and even extraordinary times are both open to question and may not permit easy answers, but public financing of campaigns is likely to help. Whether we as citizens are willing to focus and put in the effort to do better as citizens and electors remains to be seen. *The analysis also raises questions about whether we will support our representatives, once elected, in their effort to do the good and what affects that, and so it raises profoundly important questions about us.*

More Puzzles of Representative Government

In this country we have a system of legislative accountability. We are supposed to be able to hold our legislators accountable for their actions. Close examination has shown and will show that both for Congress as a whole and for the individual representative this is more difficult and more problematic than it seems.

As argued earlier, how can a citizen hold Congress as a whole responsible and how can the American people hold Congress collectively responsible when each voter is only voting for 1 or 2 members of a 535-person Congress. It is much easier to hold the president responsible for failures of government by voting for or against him or his party in an election. In principle, if you knew the majority party that controlled each house of Congress and you knew what each house had done at least in general terms, which is asking a lot of the ordinary voter, you could vote for or against that party's congressional candidate in House and Senate elections, but do most Americans act that way today? Apparently not. People who are upset with the government and the way things are going may vote against the president's party, but generally do not vote against the majority party that controls Congress when it is the opposition party. Most Americans, if they like their incumbent, and most do, vote for him. They do not blame him for the failures of Congress or the government or, for that matter, for the failures or shortcomings of the majority party in Congress.

How then do the American people hold Congress collectively responsible? The swing in party control in Congress after an election, which is the shift in seats held by Republicans and Democrats, is affected by the president's popularity, which is affected by the state of the economy, in particular, by the change in per capita income over the election year. If the president has strong approval ratings and the economy is good, his party will benefit.[26] If he has weak approval ratings, it will suffer. This makes sense in united government, when the same party controls the White House and both houses of Congress, since one can blame a Congress controlled by the president's party as well as the president, but makes less sense in divided government when at least one of the houses of Congress is controlled by a party different from that of the president. For example, if a Republican president is blocked by a Democratic Congress and cannot do what he thinks will make the country better off because he cannot pass major legislation he seeks, why should his party in the Congress, a minority party there, be blamed? Sensible or not, this is what happens. Of course, members of Congress, sensing unhappiness with the government and the state of the country, may and often do try to change policy in light of popular unhappiness, especially on the big issues. On the other hand, if the other party, not the president's party, controls Congress and if they feel the president and his party will be blamed for an unpopular state of affairs, they may have less incentive to pass legislation that will make things better. The result of all this is that the public's holding Congress collectively responsible, in light of how it acts, is less doable and easy than one might think.

In light of the public's limited knowledge of incumbents as well as the non-competitiveness of most congressional districts, it is evident that most representatives, if one looks at their behavior, are hypervigilant and almost paranoid when it comes to their reelection and thus go out of their way to bolster their support, which has a double and somewhat contradictory effect. It can make them not only better representatives of most of their supporters and potential supporters, but also more supportive of certain moneyed interests. A certain amount of paranoia, a concern and fear of how the voters will react to what they do, facilitates our republican (representative) system. Perhaps more important, even when only about a tenth of congressional districts are competitive, if one party has a ten-seat majority in the House and if the competitive seats are equally divided between the parties, the other party would have to win slightly more than seven of ten competitive seats to become the new majority.[27] A change in the majority of one house can make a great difference in what happens governmentally so that even if most incumbents are relatively invulnerable because of their behavior, resources, and other advantages, party control and thus government policy can be affected in dramatic ways. This gives the American people some control over what happens in Congress and government since the people can cause a change in party control of government and, to some extent, what government does, which allows some collective congressional accountability in a way that is important. Because the parties understand this, they have an even greater incentive to be responsive both to the people *and* to moneyed interests, the latter because it affects what the people are exposed to in campaigns. Of course, what Congress does to win and keep the support of moneyed interests often does not serve the people. These are two real, but somewhat inconsistent pulls on Congress.

Why Achieving the Collective Responsibility of Congress Is Important

Americans like and approve of their individual representatives, but generally give Congress a significantly lower approval rating. If citizens like their individual representatives, but not what Congress does, there is a way in which our government is not working. Somehow the people have to be able to hold Congress collectively responsible. If Congress is really not doing what they want and this is evidenced in its low approval rating, the people have to either get Congress to change what it is doing or change the makeup of Congress. Fortunately the people do have this power, within limits, through our parties. When party control changes in Congress, what Congress does changes, so party control is very important. On the other hand, there are forces that work against holding Congress collectively responsible through party swings. A major one is the great success rate of House and Senate incumbents seeking reelection. This reflects the demographics of House districts as well as the difficulty challengers have in raising enough money to have a chance at getting elected. The non-competitiveness of House districts not only occurs because of the natural demographics of those districts, but also because of the way state legislatures draw districts. Parties controlling various state legislatures gerrymander these districts in an effort to affect party control of the Congress and the state congressional delegation. Each party sees the other doing this in various states, which only encourages them to do the same.

Notwithstanding the factors that limit party swings, even if party swings are small, if the two houses are closely divided, small swings can change party control, as we have seen. The question remains, does this produce a way for the people to hold Congress collectively responsible? Insofar as the party swing in Congress is related to frustration with the president and his party, it is a way for the public to signal Congress it wants a change and a way for the people to hold Congress collectively responsible for its actions, especially on the large matters that affect party swing, the state of the economy and whether we are at war or peace and how that is perceived. It is interesting to ask what collective responsibility exists when the country is closely divided, as it was in the elections of 2000 and 2002. If the people are about equally divided about what direction they want Congress and the government to go, one might think the president and Congress would seek the swing or moderate vote, both in the public and Congress, which could produce a more moderate course. However, this has not happened in recent times. Rather, when one party has commanded a narrow majority in Congress, even after a very close congressional and presidential election, it has done everything it could to pass a strong and partisan agenda, the George W. Bush presidency being a prime example. Because of gerrymandering and the fact that the vast majority of districts are not competitive, parties are more partisan than they might otherwise be and less likely to cooperate, compromise, and go after the swing vote in their district because they don't need to. In addition, representatives' greatest challenges may occur in primaries, not the general election, which moves them more right or left, depending on whether they are Republican or Democrat as they try to fend off primary challenges.[28] Another factor that leads to greater partisanship, even in a closely divided Congress and after a close election, is historical. Often when a party has lacked control of both branches of government for a number of years and then gains working control, they will make great efforts to pass the biggest priority items on their agenda. This often happens even if they have no mandate to do this. Of course, it is not a requirement of democracy and republican government that officeholders always do all that the people want and nothing they do not want. There is room for the judgment of representatives as to what is the public interest, whether their voters realize what that public interest is or not. Of course, democracy requires that citizens be able to hold their individual representatives accountable for what they have done. Holding Congress collectively responsible for the state of affairs and for governmental policy means holding Congress accountable, not just holding your own representative accountable, and our party system is critical in this. Without this citizen capability, something would be seriously missing from our democratic system.

How difficult is it for voters to hold Congress collectively responsible? What additional obstacles have to be overcome? To do this, particularly if one wants Congress to do something different from what has been done, it helps if one party has a working majority in both houses and control of the White House. Because of the filibuster in the Senate, a working majority there usually requires close to a sixty-vote majority. While members are free to deviate from their party and do break party ranks more than in most parliamentary systems, party unity has been quite high since the late 1980s and so working majorities have occurred on many issues. We cannot achieve the collective responsibility of our legislative bodies as readily as some parliamentary systems can, but we probably better represent individual constituencies than they do because we don't require complete party discipline.[29] In any case through our parties we do achieve the collective responsibility of Congress on many of the big issues that citizens care about, particularly the state of the economy. For example, when people were dissatisfied with the economy under the first President Bush, they elected a Democratic president and Congress, who felt the obligation to try to do something about the economy and were in a position to do so through the passage of legislation, in Clinton's case, a major deficit reduction in 1993.

How to Get More Good People to Go into Politics

Because the president and Congress sometimes do act in the public interest, even when the action is unpopular or not being called for by the people, and because they have the leeway to do so, it is important to elect good people to public office. How do we get such people to run and how do we elect them? It is not difficult to see what discourages them. Cynicism and skepticism toward government and politics clearly discourage public service. If you think government can't do much, that politics is corrupt and self-serving, and that these things won't change, why should a good man or woman run? The need to raise money and be constantly raising it also discourages good people. Cynical, self-serving people without principles will be far less daunted by these considerations. The degree to which your private life is examined also discourages people from running as does the sacrifice your family life will have to make because of the demands of politics. On the other hand, ideas and causes can get good people to run, and some are also motivated by duty.

If citizens realized that politics was not just a spectator sport, but requires something beyond that and more than uninformed voting, and if the media profited less from treating politics and government as entertainment, especially with its emphasis on flaws and partisan conflict, then perhaps more good people would run. Many people don't like partisan conflict, but it is critical to democracy. If people understood what politics is for, what its purpose is, they might be more tolerant of conflict. In any case, many people are turned off by this and would not consider running for office. If money were not such a major element in gaining and keeping office, more good people would run.

Making media news coverage less focused on entertainment is a very difficult goal as most media are commercial enterprises. Is it possible to make programs on most commercial networks more interesting, entertaining, and informative while doing justice to politics and government? The clear answer is yes. There are ways to pique the curiosity and interest of viewers while also helping them have greater insight into politics and policy. Discussion of the issues and of politics itself can be very interesting. Explaining the issues and pointing out what needs to be understood to decide them, including through a discussion with a live audience, and then showing how demagogic politics can gloss over, ignore, or distort these key choices can be interesting. Showing how citizens' knowledge and ignorance affect their understanding of the issues could be engaging and eye-opening to people. Looking at how politics contributes to the people's knowledge and ignorance is also interesting. So is looking at the ethical choices involved in dealing with these issues and making judgments about how to deal with uncertainty. In doing this one not only entertains viewers and listeners but develops their skills as citizens. This requires sophisticated analysts, but is definitely doable. The best teachers of American politics do it all the time. At the same time, we must ask the question, will people have to believe something positive can come from this to *sustain* their interest? Besides, how long can their interest be sustained? The way twenty-four-hour news cable television networks operate now, getting people on opposite sides who try to knock the other down, often in demagogic ways, does not do the job. This may be entertainment for the viewers, but it encourages cynicism and skepticism and does not encourage the careful evaluation of one's own views. Of course, there is a connection between the perceived importance of events, for example, 9/11 and the wars in Afghanistan and Iraq, and our interest in quality news. When we think something important is at stake, which is how most Americans felt after 9/11, we want better quality news coverage. In sum while excellent analysis could grab viewers, it is not clear how long this could be sustained. It is very much an open question whether the suggestions made here could grab the attention of enough viewers to change public attitudes toward and interest in government, politics, and public service in a sustained way. This may simply be a limitation of democracy, one we accept because we value democracy.

It of course is true that government and politics have unpleasant sides, and these must be revealed as well. If one reveals the good and the bad, will that motivate more good people to get into politics? Needless to say, people of various sorts may be attracted to politics and it is not clear the good people will prevail. We have to try to better present politics and government in order to see what actually happens, and this is an experiment that could be done and is worth doing. If one raises the sophistication of citizens, will that raise the level of discourse in the media and politics? It could, though there are always ways to demagogue an issue and sometimes that is more entertaining than a good analysis, so it is not certain what the effect will be with a more sophisticated public or even whether it is possible to achieve this.[30] If this only works for a limited part of the population, so be it. While some media will seek to find or create a more sophisticated audience, others will dumb down their coverage, and appeals will be made to particular audiences as now.

For good people to run they have to believe in public service and believe it can make a positive difference. Many people don't believe that. In fact there are examples of public service and people making a positive difference, yet people don't see this and don't want to believe it.[31] Why is that? Is it because they are skeptical and cynical and find skepticism and cynicism comforting enough most of the time, except when they perceive a real crisis like 9/11, or is it because they don't want to be gullible and disappointed? Is it because they're too selfish to get involved and their skepticism and cynicism rationalizes their non-involvement? It is interesting that the people almost always attribute selfish private motives to politicians. Is this a case of projective identification, that is, are they without realizing it attributing their own selfish private motives to those who hold political office? It is likely skepticism and cynicism have multiple causes, some of which we have mentioned here.

Are people reluctant to run for public office because they recognize they have no chance to attain certain political positions without money and do not want to have such a large part of their task involve asking for money? We can do some things to remove the obstacles that prevent good people from running, for example, publicly financing congressional campaigns.

If representatives and the leeway they have are important to our political system, to what extent do we depend on the quality of leadership we have, not only in the representatives themselves, but also in the president? We take that up next.

Notes

1. David R. Mayhew, *Congress: The Electoral Connection* (New Haven, CT: Yale University Press, 1974); R. Kent Weaver, *Automatic Government* (Washington, DC: The Brookings Institution, 1988).

2. Sidney Waldman, "How Congress Does the Difficult," *PS: Political Science and Politics* XXXIII, no. 4 (December, 2000): 803–808.

3. Bob Woodward, *The Agenda* (New York: Simon & Schuster, 1994), 285.

4. Mayhew, *Congress: The Electoral Connection*, 53–54.

5. This was true both for House and Senate incumbents. Whether they agreed or disagreed with a vote on a particular bill was asked only about House incumbents.

6. Gary C. Jacobson, *The Politics of Congressional Elections*, 5th ed. (New York: Longman, 2001), 126.

7. Jacobson, *Politics of Congressional Elections*, 113–15.

8. Erich Fromm, *Escape from Freedom* (New York: Avon Books, 1941), 55.

9. Most of these findings on congressional elections come from Gary Jacobson, *Politics of Congressional Elections*.

10. Jacobson, *Politics of Congressional Elections*, 41–44.

11. Jacobson, *Politics of Congressional Elections*, 153.

12. Having non-partisan panels in states, rather than state legislatures, do congressional districting, as is done in Iowa with the result of competitive congressional districts in that state, would make these districts more competitive as would having a panel of retired judges do the districting.

13. Jeffrey H. Birnbaum and Alan S. Murray, *Showdown at Gucci Gulch: Lawmakers, Lobbyists, and the Unlikely Triumph of Tax Reform* (New York: Vintage, 1987), 127, 285.

14. Earl Blumenauer and Jim Leach, "Redistricting, a Bipartisan Sport," *New York Times*, 8 July 2003, A23.

15. All these examples of how Congress achieves leeway for itself and other examples not presented here are discussed in greater detail in Waldman, "Congress Does the Difficult," 803–808.

16. Waldman, "Congress Does the Difficult," 804.

17. R. Douglas Arnold, *The Logic of Congressional Action* (New Haven, CT: Yale University Press, 1990), 100–101.

18. Arnold, *Logic of Congressional Action*, 178–82.

19. Arnold, *Logic of Congressional Action*, 180.

20. Richard F. Fenno Jr. *Home Style: House Members in Their Districts* (Boston: Little, Brown, 1978), 151.

21. Arnold, *Logic of Congressional Action*, 181.

22. Arnold, *Logic of Congressional Action*, 181.

23. Arnold, *Logic of Congressional Action*, 182.

24. Jacobson, *Politics of Congressional Elections*, 154.

25. Arnold, *Logic of Congressional Action*, 179.

26. Jacobson, *Politics of Congressional Elections*, 154.

27. It makes a great deal of difference what percent of the competitive seats are held by the majority party. For example, if the Republicans had a ten-seat majority but also held three-fourths of the competitive seats, the Democrats would only have to win 48 percent of the competitive seats, for example all eleven of the competitive seats they held plus ten others, to become the new majority. Consequently there is an enormous incentive in each party to reduce the number of competitive seats they have, which is a great additional incentive to gerrymander congressional districts since control of the government may well be at stake. Unfortunately the Supreme Court has not been able or willing to limit gerrymandering effectively in this age of computers, which makes it much easier to do than it used to be.

28. Blumenauer and Leach, "Redistricting," A23.

29. Since the 1980s party discipline has grown in the Congress for a variety of reasons, including developments in campaign finance, changes in the demographics of House districts due to congressional redistricting by partisan state legislatures, and developments in party leadership techniques. On the latter see Barbara Sinclair, *Unorthodox Lawmaking*, 2nd ed. (Washington, DC: Congressional Quarterly Press, 2000).

30. Notice that a more sophisticated public is not the same as a more knowledgeable public. People can be more knowledgeable and still subject to demagoguery.

31. Waldman, "Congress Does the Difficult," 803–808.

~

CHAPTER THREE

The Possibilities and Limits of Presidential and Political Leadership

If representatives and the leeway they have are important to our political system, to what extent do they and we depend on the quality of leadership we have, not only in congressional representatives themselves, but also in the president, who often sets the agenda for Congress and the American people?

To assess the importance of leadership and its limits, we might begin by asking what our leader, the president, is supposed to do. Clearly the president has numerous responsibilities, but one of his most important tasks is to help us answer the question, who are we, in the sense of what do we stand for and what do we need to do in light of what we stand for.[1] Of course, the president does not always have to pose fundamental questions about our polity or policy, but when we are not who we say we are and when our society has fundamental flaws inconsistent with who we say we are, the president faces the challenge of helping us see what we have not done and how we can do it. Whether he takes up that challenge and should is one of the most important decisions he faces, and we will examine some of the considerations involved in that decision.

Democratic government, like all government, exists not only to settle certain things, but to deal with some of the fundamental problems of the society and economy. Often transactional politics does much of the ordinary work of politics, but sometimes transformational politics is required.[2] Transactional politics ordinarily occurs in times of stability and involves the bargaining we are familiar with and which Richard Neustadt has described very well.[3] Transformational politics involves something more. Often to solve fundamental problems in our society government needs to be transformational. Lincoln during the Civil War and Roosevelt in the Depression exemplify two transformational presidencies. In both cases moral leadership was critical in changing the country and its citizens, and we shall argue that this is usually the case in transformational politics. What is involved in such leadership will become clear as we examine these cases.

"Transforming leaders articulate and reinterpret the historical situation in times of uncertainty."[4] Franklin Roosevelt in the Depression, Lincoln in the Civil War, Roosevelt after Pearl Harbor, and George W. Bush after 9/11 are all examples of transforming leaders in times of uncertainty. In these potentially transforming times leaders appeal to revised versions of our fundamental moral and political beliefs and values, revised because they're being reapplied to new situations involving where we are, what has happened, and where we want to go. Hargrove says this is the only way to close the gap between presidential weakness and presidential aspiration, an aspiration to solve certain extremely important or fundamental problems we face.[5] After World War II presidents such as Truman, Eisenhower, and Kennedy did this in seeking the support and resolve of the American people in the Cold War. Johnson tried to do this in dealing with Vietnam, but the American people eventually lost patience with that war as victory eluded America.

To achieve the deepest aspirations of our culture the leader has to engage in transformational politics by evoking these aspirations "in a manner that tells the truth about the practical steps needed to fulfill them."[6] Lincoln did this at Gettysburg when he said,

> Our fathers brought forth upon this continent a new nation, conceived in Liberty, and dedicated to the proposition that all men are created equal. . . . It is rather for us to be here dedicated to the great task remaining before us . . . that the nation shall, under God, have a new birth of freedom, and that the government of the people, by the people, and for the people, shall not perish from the earth.[7]

Some might argue that George W. Bush tried to evoke our deepest aspirations in dealing with education through his No Child Left Behind legislation, but he did so without success because he did not describe or propose the practical steps that would achieve this or likely even make significant progress toward this goal. If Bush had told the truth about what was required to achieve this or even a significant part of it, Americans would not want to hear it nor would they support it. We simply were unwilling to devote the resources required to achieve this. Either Bush did not know what was required for education to work for everyone, "to leave no child behind," or, more likely, he thought it impossible for political or economic or ideological reasons to commit the resources to do this so he did not propose what would do the job. Bush may well have seen his work as incremental, but will his goal be achieved that way? In politics you do what you can, but sometimes that will not get the job done.

Leaders "who would appeal to popular majorities" must "discern and evoke unresolved problems and suggest plausible remedies that reinterpret shared beliefs and values in new, appropriate ways."[8] But what if the people don't see or care about those problems or don't believe the problems can be solved and cannot be changed in their views during the tenure of the leader or for the foreseeable future? Then the problems cannot be evoked, which limits the influence of plausible remedies, if any are suggested. The people's beliefs and values do not connect with these problems, and this limits leadership and what the country can do. It limits the country. It is easy to say that it is the job of the president to change that, to get us to see what we need to see, but often that is impossible and saying the job of the president is to change us is a way of passing the buck. While President Harry S Truman may have had a sign on his desk that said, "the buck stops here," in reality on important questions the buck often stops not at the president's desk, but with us.

Reinterpreting and applying the peoples' values to critical problems is hard because citizens have to really care, which is the hard part. They have to get it. Of course, sometimes this is easier than at other times. For example, Franklin Roosevelt sold the New Deal by pointing out the ways in which the Depression threatened the general welfare and corporations threatened economic individualism. To quote from his 1936 Convention speech,

> The royalists of the economic order have conceded that political freedom was the business of the Government, but they have maintained that economic slavery was nobody's business. They granted that the Government could protect the citizen in his right to vote, but they denied that the Government could do anything to protect the citizen in his right to work and his right to live. Today we stand committed to the proposition that freedom is no half-and-half affair. If the average citizen is guaranteed equal opportunity in the polling place, he must have equal opportunity in the market place.[9]

In selling the Great Society Lyndon Johnson spoke about helping people help themselves. As he said in his "We Shall Overcome" speech to Congress on March 15, 1965, "I want to be the President who educated young children

. . . who helped to feed the hungry . . .who helped the poor to find their own way."[10]

"Clearly the leader who commands compelling causes has an extraordinary personal influence over his followers."[11] But what if some of the largest problems facing the country are not compelling causes to the public? This often is the case. Politicians face this regularly, and they usually respond by trimming their sails. We can ask whether a leader can make a cause compelling that isn't compelling to the public. It certainly is far from easy and often not possible. Even our greatest leaders had trouble with this. One can see that in all the difficulties Franklin Roosevelt had in getting Americans to take the threat of Adolph Hitler seriously in the middle and late 1930s and in the difficulty Lincoln had with the border states and the issue of slavery.[12] This means that we the people often ultimately determine what this country does in solving some of our most important problems.

Leadership is clearly linked to collective purpose.[13] But what are our collective purposes, our real ones, not just ones we mouth? That is another way we are absolutely critical to what happens. Of course, politicians can do more than represent the views citizens currently have. They can decide what challenges they will present to the public in an attempt to influence those views, but the public has to respond to those challenges. Here our self-love can affect matters. If we do not see and do not care about the plight of certain people in our country, then a president's challenge to us to support action to relieve their plight can fall on deaf ears and blind eyes.

Since we have and will focus on the importance of and problems caused by self-love in political life, we need to say something about it. Self-love can be defined as "regard for oneself and one's own interest."[14] There is nothing wrong with this in itself, in fact it likely has positive consequences in life, and self-love often involves trying to do things for one's family as well as oneself. The problem occurs when this focus on yourself and your interests is exclusive and excessive. One way the idea of needed balance is captured can be seen in the saying, "If I am not for myself, who will be for me? If not now, when? If I am only for myself, what am I?"[15] This saying can allow us to see the connection between self-love and selfishness. Selfish can be defined as "too much concerned with one's own welfare or interests and having little or no concern for others." In this work we shall use the term self-love, a term from *The Federalist Papers*, rather than the term selfish, and we shall mean by it excessive self-love, a self-love that doesn't take adequate account of the needs of others beyond oneself and one's family.

If ideas are be resources for social action, they must express the felt necessities of people's lives.[16] Thus what people are feeling and experiencing in their lives strongly influences politics. If people feel the absence of needed healthcare in their lives, then healthcare has a political opening. But if people do not feel that necessity, then the going is tougher. While the leader(s) can propose ideas that are congruent with the ideas people hold or can come to hold and congruent with conditions and while the leader's creativity and energy are also critical to success, a real opportunity for change must be there.[17] Opportunity is not always there. Again one sees this in Roosevelt's frustrations in getting Americans to face the threat of Nazism in the mid to late 1930s and in Lincoln's caution and fear of alienating the border states and thus losing the Civil War by emancipating the slaves a year or two before he did it.

Leaders can attempt to teach deep moral truths, for example, Lincoln at Gettysburg when he zeroed in on the Declaration of Independence's focus on the equality of all, a focus that had been abandoned in the Constitution.[18] But when leaders do this, will citizens be receptive to these truths *and* be prepared to support action on their behalf?[19] *Leaders can only teach deep moral truths if the people are receptive. Once again, the people's morality is critical in affecting what happens.*

Of course, leaders can act in another way. They can take ethnic identities and tribal ones and put people at odds in order to secure power and position. Yugoslavia (Milosevic), Nigeria, Rwanda, and the Middle East are just some of the places that illustrate this, and it could happen anywhere including this country. This again shows the importance of morals and purpose because when they are absent or wrongly conceived, bad things can happen.

Leadership involves both what the president can do and how the public will respond to his efforts. How the public responds often is as much about the public as it is about the leader. From that perspective it is interesting to ask, when do people agree that something is a critical problem so that they're prepared to support the government in dealing with it and when do they say, you'll have to convince me your way of dealing with this important problem will work and will be worth the costs. Often when the problem is military, particularly an attack on our shores as with the 9/11 attack, the people seem to understand the problem is significant and are prepared to follow their leader in what he proposes to do to deal with it. Basically they want their leader to take care of them and handle the problem, and thus they support the leader. One can see this in the initial support both for the war with Afghanistan and with Iraq. If the problem seems to be solved or significantly reduced, as they judge matters, the support continues. In contrast, when it comes to dealing with failing schools, most people may abstractly or cognitively realize this is a problem, but they do not experience or feel it in the same way they do a terrorist or a military threat and are less supportive of policies that are required to improve this situation significantly. They may tolerate efforts to improve education at failing schools, but usually are less likely to support devoting the resources required to make significant progress in solving the problem and more quickly tire of a focus on it. Presumably this is because they feel failed education is less of a problem for them since it is not their children who are not getting educated. *Thus how we experience realities and whether we care about the fate of others are absolutely critical to our reactions toward particular problems the country faces and what we are willing to support to deal with them. This is a critical reality of democracy, which we often obscure with our focus on the weaknesses of politicians and certain aspects of our political system.*

Clearly in democratic politics the interpretations of reality given by leaders are assessed by others, who may or may not buy them. Figuring out the bases of the peoples' assessments and what affects them should be a critical part of the study of politics. Because people often focus on their own problems, for example, their own kids' education, they focus less on the education of others outside of the community where they live, including those who are more deprived economically and disadvantaged in other ways. If people care less about a particular problem, they are moved less by proposed plausible remedies to solve that problem. They also will be moved less by conflict focusing on that problem.[20]

Citizens may not want to face reality or they may fear facing it and its significance.[21] If people recognized, even vaguely, how much it would cost to transform the communities that house poor schools as part of an effort to improve those schools and the difficulty of that venture, they likely would not want to face the problems of those schools. Another example of this desire to avoid facing reality was the reluctance of Europeans and Americans in the 1930s to respond to or even recognize the Nazi threat. In light of the latter experience the leaders of the Western powers consciously developed the concept of the Cold War so that they with the support of their people would be ready to do whatever it took to oppose the expansion of communism. Clearly our political leaders have not used their capital in the same way to try to deal with the problem of education. Why? Because it has not been a high enough priority, and other problems have taken precedence such as the economy, jobs, Social Security, Medicare, and the war on terrorism. This of course reflects public opinion, which affects what politicians do in the effort to garner and maintain support and affects which problems leaders focus on and emphasize to the public. In the case of the Cold War presidents made the judgment that they had to make the people see the dangers involved and support necessary action to oppose those dangers. In the case of education for our poorest students and our worst and failing schools this has not been done. This not only reflects a difference in priorities, but a political judgment that the public had to be and could be mobilized on the one issue and not the other. In many instances one should not criticize political leaders for this by saying they are too dependent on polls and focus groups. Without public support it is extremely difficult for leaders to move on very difficult and costly projects, and it is often impossible for leaders to get the public to care about something large they currently don't care about or see something they don't want to see. One sees this in Franklin Roosevelt, who had great fears about losing the American people if he pushed them too hard about the threat he thought Adolph Hitler posed. He hoped events would teach them what he alone couldn't and when he had to, he went around Congress and the American people in the desperate days of 1940 and 1941.[22] Of course, any leader could in principle say whatever he wishes and push whatever projects he thought most important, regardless of their cost and difficulty, but could he maintain the support of the Congress and the people? Most leaders rather choose to achieve what they think they must *and* can while trying, at the same time, to maintain public support. Some, of course, are feistier than others and are more willing to lose the support of the people, for example Harry Truman, but what Truman achieved was limited, especially in domestic policy. Most leaders have occasional issues where they are willing to use up much of their political credit, but these issues usually concern matters of national security. Somehow education for the poor does not meet that hurdle as most see matters. In any case, whatever price the president is willing to pay, if he does not have Congress and the people behind him, what he can achieve is limited.

Can the president make us care about what we do not really care about? It is doubtful. A president regularly talking about the importance of failed education and proposing to devote enormous resources to deal with it would not likely win our support or Congress's. What is lacking is in us. He cannot put there what is not there. On defense he can play to our fears about our security, on Medicare and Social Security he can play on the fact that we will be old someday and want that assistance, but he has no similar move he can make on the subject of failed education, which primarily affects the poor and minorities. There are a number of important problems like that where what he can do is limited. Just as he cannot make us see the situation of certain people in our country, he cannot make us see how the fate of people around the world can ultimately affect us, and this is true even after September 11th. He cannot do much to make us much more moral or compassionate. We, of course, often want to blame the president and our political leaders for the unresolved problems in this country and even for our national faults and shortcomings, that is when we are not blaming the victims of these problems and shortcomings, but we often are the ones who limit what our political leaders can do. Of course, they will very rarely point that out because in so doing they set themselves up for criticism of the following sort, "You have not been a good leader. The problem is not with the American people. It is with our leaders and politicians." This was a major reaction to Jimmy Carter's Malaise speech in the late 1970s. Nevertheless, in an area such as failed education for the poor, the problem is due to us, not our leaders, since they cannot get us to do what we need to do. Leaders balance purpose and prudence to deal with the possibilities that exist in a political context.[23] That is why they don't attempt certain things, which we sometimes criticize them for, but the fault and responsibility are ultimately ours. Thus, once again morality and what affects it are critical to politics.

Leaders should "teach reality" by evoking our deepest aspirations, the deepest aspirations of our culture, in a way that describes the practical steps needed to fulfill these in confronting particular problems.[24] However, citizens often don't want to hear this when it comes to particular challenges. Of course, what we are ready to hear and see can change over time, sometimes at least partly because of the actions of the leader, whose success often depends on events and his use of events. Lincoln illustrates this when in 1862 he used the military difficulties the Union was having in the Civil War and the need for additional manpower to justify his executive order as Commander-in-Chief to emancipate the slaves.

Hargrove importantly sees that political leadership should be and often is moral agency.[25] Hargrove focuses on moral leadership because he sees its necessity and its reality. Without it the president cannot do what he needs to do and should do. Bargaining alone cannot get the job done when it comes to certain matters. But once one sees the need for moral leadership, one sees the need for cultural leadership, to which we now turn.

Cultural Leadership

The central task of political leadership is cultural interpretation, a focus on who we are and what we believe in and care about.[26] Consequently we need to look at American political culture, even if briefly, since this provides both resources and the constraints on leadership. Culture and values affect what leaders and citizens can do, do, and what they will not do.

Liberalism, evident in our emphasis on the market and on economic individualism, characterizes our cultural context, but so does democratic individualism, which focuses on the inequality created by the market and our efforts to deal with that.[27] Both have been characterized as liberalism. While this is a helpful orientation, I analyze and explain American politics in terms of self-love and the need to correct for it. What is the significance of this difference? The differences between these two orientations are not great as these are two ways of getting at the same thing though probably the formulation of self-love goes deeper. That conception is closer to that found in religion and philosophy and, most important, gives a moral edge to the analysis, which is needed.

What else can we see in our culture? Culturally we value liberty, freedom, and equality of opportunity. Freedom includes choosing between right and wrong, not just doing your own thing and being what you can be, and for all these reasons responsibility is related to freedom. We clearly do not believe in "equality" of opportunity in the sense of seeking complete equality of opportunity, in part because obtaining it is impossible and also because many of us believe it is justifiable to give one's children advantages if we can, even if not every child has those advantages. What then do we mean by equality of opportunity, a notion most of us take seriously? We believe in opportunity for people though we mean different things by that. A belief in opportunity rather than equality of opportunity may be a more accurate representation of our beliefs. Many of us accept the idea of some minimum or adequate opportunity that all people should have. Our leaders draw on these ideas in their efforts to influence us, and they can be constrained as well as facilitated by them.

Since the public is critical to presidential leadership and to solving certain important problems facing our country, we need to look more closely at the public, which is our next topic.

Notes

1. Erwin C. Hargrove, *The President as Leader* (Lawrence: University Press of Kansas, 1998), 44.

2. Hargrove, *The President*, 47.

3. Richard E. Neustadt, *Presidential Power and Modern Presidents* (New York: Free Press, 1990).

4. Hargrove, *The President*, 30.

5. Hargrove, *The President*, 30–47.

6. Hargrove, *The President*, 47.

7. Gary Wills, *Lincoln at Gettysburg* (New York: Simon & Schuster, 1992), 261.

8. Hargrove, *The President*, 25.

9. James MacGregor Burns, *The Lion and the Fox* (New York: Harcourt, Brace, 1957), 274.

10. Doris Kearns Goodwin, *Lyndon Johnson and the American Dream* (New York: St. Martin's Griffin, 1976), 230.

11. James MacGregor Burns, *Leadership* (New York: Harper & Row, 1975), 34.

12. Burns, *The Lion and the Fox.*

13. Burns, *Leadership*, 3, 389.

14. Victoria Neufeldt, ed. *Webster's New World College Dictionary*, 3rd ed. (New York: Macmillan, 1997).

15. Mishnah, Avot 1:14

16. Neustadt, *Presidential Power*, 80–90.

17. Hargrove, *The President*, 40.

18. Wills, *Lincoln at Gettysburg.*

19. Hargrove, *The President*, 38–42, calls this cultural leadership.

20. This is a problem with the argument that the weak can be served by a democratizing process mobilized by conflict.

21. Hargrove, *The President*, 46.

22. Burns, *The Lion and the Fox.*

23. Hargrove, *The President*, 41.

24. Hargrove, *The President*, 42–46.

25. Hargrove, *The President*, 44.

26. Hargrove, *The President*, 49–75.

27. Hargrove, *The President*, 52.

∼

The Public: An Analysis of Us and What That Means for American Democracy

The Role of the Public in Affecting What Problems Government Can Solve: Education as a Case Study

We have seen how our representatives have leeway in acting and thus have seen the potential importance of morality in affecting how they use that leeway. We have also seen how leadership, even transformational leadership, requires that we respond to moral appeals from the leader and thus have seen again the importance of our morality in affecting what our country can achieve. We now turn to the public to see how it affects what this country can achieve. We do so by looking at education as a case study to see what the role of the public is in affecting what problems government can solve.

If we are to evaluate our political system and our politicians, we need to ask what the most important problems are that our country faces. Those who look at America will be aware of our poverty and race problems, particularly the problems of those who are unemployed long-term; those who are single parents, including at young ages; those who are involved in crime, especially drug-related crime; and those who work but not for a living wage. Clearly the failure of education can be tied to these problems, both as their effect and cause in a self-perpetuating pattern. We know or should know that our poorest schools are not giving our least achieving students the education they need to have a reasonable chance to better their lot in life. For example, black and Hispanic twelfth-grade students scored below the level

45

of proficiency achieved, on average, by white children in the seventh grade.[1] The question facing America, surely one of the greatest domestic policy questions, is whether we can solve this problem. While Americans pay lip service to education and opportunity for all, they primarily care about education for their own children. When they respond to education issues, they think mostly about their own communities. While this is reasonable, it is not enough as it ignores education in poor communities. The consequence of most citizens not really caring about education for poor kids is that what our national and state leaders propose to deal with this problem is very limited and will not get the job done. For example, George W. Bush's focus on annual tests measuring proficiency was meant to lead to the identification of failing schools that as a last resort would be closed down and reopened under new leadership, but that will not get the job done without sufficient additional resources. The goal of his legislation was the proficiency of every child in ten to twelve years, but there is no way that will happen through the means he and Congress passed. Under the legislation, if schools fail to improve their students' scores, students would be allowed to go to other schools in the same district, but that also will not get the job done. What will occur from this testing is that we will identify by race, ethnic group, and income which students are not progressing, which we already know. Will this make Americans more concerned with and sympathetic to this problem? It is doubtful it will. In fact, citizens could come to believe the problem is hopeless, as some already do, blame the families of these kids and their culture, or be satisfied with improving the lot of only a few, perhaps through a voucher system, all of which are the easier answers. What is clear is that, as of now, the country is not prepared to do what it will take to get the job done. Little is being done to alter class size, build new and repair old facilities, pay teachers more, recruit and train better teachers, and, most important, improve the places where these kids live, for example, by improving the employment picture for people in their community and all that would follow from that. The solutions proposed by the government are inadequate not only because the problem is difficult but also because our society has not faced up to what is required to make things better and has not made the needed commitment. This hampers what our leaders can propose and what our representatives can achieve. When someone comes along and thinks big about such problems, as Bill Bradley attempted in his failed presidential campaign of 2000, it does not grab people. They did not care enough about this agenda and didn't believe his vision, either in the sense of wanting to make the needed commitment to achieve it or believing it was doable. The result of this is a significantly limited political agenda and limited achievement, which then limits what our citizens expect of government in this area and what our leaders try to do. The focus instead is how we make our own local school systems better, which doesn't do the job for the poor districts. We see failed efforts in schools after the government has spent money and say the money was wasted and think the problem is hopeless. There is no crisis most of us personally experience to force us to focus on the problem and commit to do what it takes to solve it. When failed education and limited opportunities lead to unemployment and crime, we build prisons for the criminals. We do not realize that we share responsibility for the failures of education because we are limited in what we are willing to support. We don't want to think about this and don't want to take responsibility for our part so we blame the blacks and the poor, focus on weaknesses in their culture, and blame the government, the teachers, and the bureaucracy.[2] This allows us to continue our focus on our own neighborhoods and our own parochial needs. And, of course, politicians who want our support do not point out our complicity in the failure.

What we fundamentally fail to understand and recognize is that the president and our representatives are limited in what they can achieve and that they are limited by us. If leaving no child behind, or even leaving only a few behind, were a smaller task that required far fewer financial resources, perhaps our leaders and representatives could do it without our support, but this is too big a job.

One could ask, "If this is important, why can't the president and Congress or, for that matter, governors, state legislatures, and local school districts do this? That's part of their job and if they can't do this, if it's so important, what do we need them for?" Representative government is a cooperative enterprise, especially on a big issue like this. It involves the executive, the legislature, the courts, *and the people*. Leaders need followers. "We the people" are critical. This is as true for our public ventures as for our private ones.

When a president or other political leader proposes educational reform and it fails, we blame the leader. We may also blame other officeholders. It rarely occurs to us that we are to blame because of our lack of commitment and support, which affects what leaders and representatives try to do and can do. Politicians will not tell us it is our fault because that is a sure way to lose support. We scapegoat our political leaders. We say you should have persuaded us what we need to do and how to do it. That is your job as a leader. We don't recognize that leaders cannot lead us where we will not go. Those running against current officeholders who want to criticize their failures do not point out our complicity in some of those failures. Rather, they make it seem as if they could get the job done. When they are elected, they can't, and the cycle continues. So we blame our leaders and representatives. Representative government becomes scapegoat government. Since there are always politicians criticizing those in power and office, they of course also criticize officeholders, not us. All this keeps us in darkness, not allowing us to face the part we play in the failure to solve the problem.[3]

Government as the Protector of the Weak: Can It Do the Job?

Some people, probably many if they thought about it, believe that the role of government is to protect the weaker against the stronger, not to ratify the balance of power in the private sector.[4] According to one view, this happens in a democracy when political parties and candidates, striving to win elections, frame and pose issues to grab the public's attention and be popular so that the issue framers win elections. In this way issues are brought from back rooms to the wider public where the majority determines who wins. This has been called the socialization of conflict, a process that brings in a larger audience whose majority rules. It is the function of public authority to modify private power relations by enlarging the scope of conflict. Nothing could be more mistaken than to suppose that public authority merely registers the dominance of the strong over the weak in the private sector.[5] An example of this may be civil rights in the 1960s when the federal government, with the support of national majorities, eliminated segregationist, Jim Crow laws in southern states. Democracy, it is argued, provides the public with a second power system to counterbalance economic power. Interest groups can do this when they have been on the losing side and try to get our attention by posing a conflict that will lead us to support them and what they are for. The elderly did this in the late 1980s when they objected to changes in catastrophic coverage by Medicare, which they felt would hurt other Medicare coverage.

Unfortunately there are limits to this dynamic. If the government is not seen by the people as able to solve a particular problem, for example, the problem of failing education for poor kids, then there is unlikely to be conflict over that issue with one of the two major parties proposing real solutions, and it is unlikely to be a serious major item on the agenda. Candidates who emphasize this issue, a possible example was Bill Bradley's presidential campaign in 2000, are unlikely to grab the public's attention. This illustrates the great importance of the public's skepticism of and cynicism toward government in general and on particular matters and shows that one of the most powerful things anyone can do is cause, elicit, and reinforce that skepticism and cynicism, which is exactly what conservatives on the media who oppose large government often try to do. This skepticism and cynicism may be one of the most important results of modern media coverage, whether intentional or not. While it might seem that skepticism could help the public protect itself, it likely has just the opposite effect. People who don't want or need the government to do much and who fear that government may expand its role have an incentive to put the government down and respond positively to messages that do this.

To the extent we focus on the private sector to get our rewards, we focus less on politics. The problem is that the less we focus on politics, the less well the political system functions as a second power system to balance the most powerful in the private sector. This is because less will grab our attention politically because we are otherwise occupied. As a result, this second power system is less able to balance the power system created by our market economy.

In an effort to win elections politicians and parties pose conflicts they hope will move us and lead us to support them.[6] Even when the political system works in the way Schattschneider describes, which it often does, the alternatives posed to the public are often presented very simply and in short sound bites. "Get the economy moving," "give people some control over their Social Security funds," "make schools accountable," "let people keep more of their own money to spend as they wish," "reduce the size of government," "strengthen America," "reduce the influence of special interests," and the like. These are fairly simple and general appeals. The question is whether these and similar appeals distort reality or capture enough of it to allow sensible choice. Do they empower people in facilitating their interests or, by being so general and simple, do they preclude people making intelligent choices? For example, holding schools accountable through annual testing will not produce successful schools by itself, even if failing schools are closed down and then reopened under new leadership. Giving students attending failing schools the option of going to other schools in their school district will probably not improve the achievement of most students. For one thing they may not be able to gain admission to the "better" schools in the district for space is likely to be limited. Improving the education of those low in achievement in our failing schools requires a commitment of resources to education and to the wider environment of these students far larger than what we are doing and are prepared to do. Thus, "making schools accountable" may create the illusion we are significantly trying to improve education when we have very little chance of improving education through accountability alone. In that way the appeal, making schools accountable, may mislead

since it suggests this policy will produce significantly more successful education, which is unlikely.

Of course, sometimes these types of simple appeals really allow citizens to
achieve their interests. For example, the fear that future challengers would
charge them with selling out to special interests probably created majority
support in Congress for the Reagan tax reform of 1986, which took many tax
loopholes away from special interests.[7] Given their knowledge and interest in
politics, can most citizens distinguish useful political framings from those
that are not useful and are misleading? Even on the large issues, more often
than we'd like to admit they cannot. Politicians have a term that describes
fraudulent appeals to the public. They call it "demagogic politics." This is
presenting an issue in such an oversimplified way as to distort or misrepresent
it. It also can mean playing to the emotions of the listeners in a way that gets
in the way of a reasoned consideration of the issue. It is interesting that
politicians use these words more than the public and more than the main-
stream media do. They do so because they understand better than the public
what is going on because they see it a lot.

Thus, for a variety of reasons Schattschneider's view of how politics can
help the weak does not solve all the problems. While politics can sometimes
provide a second power system for the people, they are not always empowered by it.

To what extent do we need politics to be a second power system? There
are many instances where a second power system is desirable. For example,
after the accounting frauds at Enron and World Com and their effect on
stockholders and retirement plans, politicians were pushed to act to clean up
this situation. Of course, how effective the new reforms will be depends both
on the efforts of those who wrote the reforms and perhaps on the continuing
attention of the public. Perhaps one reason the middle class is not doing
much better in real income per worker than they were in the 1970s, despite
great productivity gains and the growing wealth of the best off, is because this
second power system has not worked, perhaps because the people have not
recognized its importance given their focus on the private sector. Things
have not gotten bad enough for us to focus on rebalancing through politics.
If the middle class continues not to make progress economically, that is likely
to change. The poor need politics as a second power system even more than
the middle class, but they are often not in a good position to take advantage
of it because they simply do not have the numbers. When they can join with
the middle class or a substantial part of it politically, they are more empowered. Clearly this is not easy to pull off. Sometimes, however, in an effort to
win the support of the disadvantaged and those who care about their situa-

tion, or simply because it is the right thing to do, officeholders pass legislation intended to benefit the poor. Medicaid, aid to disadvantaged schools, and food stamps are obvious examples. What's interesting about these examples is that in every case there are interests who support this legislation that stand to benefit from it, for example, doctors, hospitals, labs, and pharmaceutical companies with Medicaid, teachers with schools, and farmers with food stamps. Because the poor often lack power, they need these allies. In any case, the poor are not in as good a position as the middle class to use politics as a second power system.

The Significance of Selfishness for Government and Politics

We have seen that the ability of our government to solve certain important problems in society is limited by the lack of support of our people, a lack due to our selfishness and self-love. It is time to ask what the effect of selfishness or self-love is on attitudes to government and politics? If you have most of what you want and believe you can continue to get it from the private sector and don't care about much else, you may not want government interfering with what you have and what you do. A cynical and skeptical attitude toward government can help you keep what you have if it leads you and others to not want government to do much. It is also true many people are spending all they have and more. They don't want their taxes going up, and they resent having to pay for others when they're working hard and feel they're barely able to pay their bills. Since they are responsible for taking care of themselves and their families, they want others to do the same so these others don't depend on them. They don't want to pay for others who aren't working. President Clinton tried to speak to this commonly held view by speaking of "people who work hard and play by the rules" and by emphasizing responsibility. Of course, if some of these same people want things from government, for example, business subsidies, their attitude is often quite different. The same people who were against national health reform in 1994, which would have insured most of the uninsured, liked Medicare. They thought Medicare benefited them or would, but insuring the uninsured would cost them money (higher taxes) and/or benefits if they were already insured, which 85 percent were. Thus when Hillary Clinton tried to counter the anti-government arguments of reform opponents by pointing out that most people liked Medicare, the argument didn't convince people since she was comparing apples and oranges, a program that helped "us" in contrast to a program that helped others (them).

To the extent that government serves the less strong and the weak, it is in the interest of the better off who are selfish and don't want to share more of the rewards of their efforts to denigrate government and make people expect less of it. If most people expect little from government, they are less likely to ask government to help them or others.

Individualism and the notion of self-reliance are critical in affecting what people think the role of government is. To the extent that people feel that whatever happens to them in life should and largely does depend on their own efforts, which is what most of us are taught, they will rely less on government and be less likely to want others to rely on government. The idea that what happens to us in life depends on our own efforts, while it contains some truth, is also absurd on its face. Where we were born in the world, into what circumstances, has an enormous impact on our fate, whatever efforts we make or do not make. This is patently true, and it is striking how often we forget or ignore this reality.

If you can persuade people that individuals are being denied "equal opportunity" or some minimum opportunity to which they think people have a right, you can sometimes convince them that government has a role to compensate for this denial of opportunity and even to change the opportunities that exist. That is what FDR did during the Depression when he said the average citizen must have equal opportunity in the market place and suggested economic royalists were preventing that.[8] It is also how LBJ tried to sell the Great Society. FDR's task was the easier one because the Depression did take away the opportunities of millions, across class, racial, and ethnic group lines, as they experienced unemployment.

People care most about how they and their families are doing, what progress they are making and expect to make. Typical citizens care less about how the rich are doing, what advantages their children have, or how the poor are making out, what disadvantages they have, than about how they and their families are doing and how they expect to do. If times are good, they may tolerate doing more for the less well off though they are unlikely to push for such action; rather, they will tolerate the initiatives of the political elite, to a limited extent. This is the lesson of Lyndon Johnson's Great Society. The Great Society included Medicare, a program that benefited all classes, as well as some assistance to the poor. Even with the Great Society, despite the prosperity of the times, people's support and tolerance of the programs were limited.[9] The urban riots, which started in Watts in the summer of 1965 and continued in other cities through the summers of 1967 and 1968, turned many Americans against the War on Poverty as more and more of our citizens began to think that blacks were "going too fast," demanding too

much. It is hard to know whether the backlash that occurred against programs for the poor and minorities would have occurred, absent the urban riots, but it was clear from the beginning of the War on Poverty that the mass
public didn't request it and basically tolerated it. If times are bad and many
people are suffering, including family members and friends, as was the case in
the Depression, people will be more open to government action to improve
their situation; in fact, they will expect and demand it. Thus, what we are,
think, and want depend on circumstances, particularly our own. It is the job
of politicians and statesmen to be opportunistic, that is, to take advantage of
the opportunities these circumstances provide, and they do.

Most Americans want to be left alone so they can pursue happiness. They
want government to handle whatever they think government "needs to handle," especially as it affects their personal welfare, and usually they do not
want to think much about this. They just want it done. Once government
passes certain benefits, such as Medicare and Social Security, which the people expect to benefit from and do, they expect the government to finance
and properly run those programs so they get their benefits. During the battle
over Clinton's healthcare reform in 1994 Newt Gingrich believed that Clinton's reform must be defeated because otherwise it would create a stronger al-
legiance to the majority Democratic Party for years.[10] Gingrich understood
that what Americans expect from government is not fixed, but depends on
what government does at various times, that is, on government policy, which
is why politicians and, for that matter, powerful interests fought so hard over
healthcare policy in 1994. Once national healthcare is provided, however it
is done, citizens come to expect it, want it, and demand reasonable service.

Often when the masses approve of particular government programs, we
see an "escape from freedom."[11] People want their leaders, whether it is the
president or other representatives, to take care of them. They usually do not
worry about how difficult it will be to do that. When that doesn't happen,
they get skeptical, cynical, and annoyed. They may well demand a change in
government and policy.

The middle class has the numbers to push for what it wants, often successfully on matters it really cares about, Social Security and Medicare being obvious examples. The rich have money, which often allows them to
lobby successfully for what they want, tax loopholes and breaks being an obvious example. The poor lack numbers and money, which is why they have
the hardest time getting what they want and why they are politically vulnerable. Of course, the Democratic Party sometimes provides benefits to the
poor for political reasons as well as reasons of belief, and sometimes the
elite, regardless of party, also supports benefits for the most disadvantaged

for moral reasons as well as to strengthen the society. Nevertheless, the poor are more politically vulnerable than the middle class or the rich. When one sees that the poor and the weak are limited in what they get politically and are the most vulnerable, one is seeing the place of self-love in our politics.

Most of us do not feel a personal need to participate in politics other than as superficial spectators most of the time, probably because we get and think we get most of the benefits we focus on from the private sector, not government, a consequence of our capitalist system. We also believe we should gain most of our benefits through our personal efforts, not through government, and we expect most of the important benefits we get from government to continue, whether we pay close attention or not. So why participate? This is a result of our culture and what we have been taught by experience and otherwise. We probably also believe that deeper and stronger political participation by us will not make much difference to what happens and what happens to us.

Because of our focus on the private sector as the source of most of our rewards, our civic engagement is very limited and we do not generally develop social trust and cooperative practices in civic action.[12] Even if social trust somehow came to exist and led to public action, we might still have many of the problems described in this work since those who worked together might still be selfish in what they sought, ignoring the needs of certain others.

Democracy's Uses

This last discussion raises interesting questions about our democracy, what is it good for and especially why do we value it, particularly since we make limited use of it most of the time? From time to time we ask some of our citizens to risk their lives for it, and many of our countrymen have made the ultimate sacrifice, but what is it we are defending? The answer to that is complicated, but perhaps part of the answer is that we want a democratic system, even if our participation in and use of it is limited most of the time, so that it is there for us when we really want to use it. If things really get bad, we want to be able to join with others to get new leaders, representatives, and policies, to get a change for the better. This potential is extremely important. But one has to ask, if we have not participated much politically, will we be able to participate wisely when we want a change? Will we be more subject to demagogic appeals because of our lack of knowledge and political experience? In times of crisis in the past we have been fortunate in our choices, Roosevelt in the Depression, Lincoln in the Civil War, but are we vulnerable to bad leaders in crises, leaders who will make bad policy choices, because of our limited involvement in ordinary times. It is certainly true that we are more subject to demagogic appeals, those that are overly simple and play on our emotions and prejudices, if we are less informed and experienced in politics. But we must also acknowledge that some who are involved in politics and somewhat knowledgeable can be moved by demagogic appeals so knowledge and experience do not guarantee invulnerability to demagogues. On the other hand, somewhat sophisticated knowledge and thoughtfulness can help us resist demagogic appeals, and that degree of knowledge and thoughtfulness is within our reach if we wish it. We do not know how subject the American people would be to demagogic appeals in times of crisis. If people fall victim to demagoguery, eventually they will discover the disasters that demagogues can cause and realize their mistake, but that can occur too late. The next election may be too late to prevent those disasters.

In discussing the uses of democracy we must also recognize that those who want change to better their situation but who are a numerical minority and are likely to remain that way, for example, the poor and, currently, racial and ethnic minorities, and who do not have the financial resources to compensate politically for their minority status, may be out of luck if the majority isn't with them, and that situation could continue for the indefinite future. This can happen even though sometimes the political system serves numerical minorities and not just the rich. Sometimes the elite, even when the majority of people are not pushing for this, becomes concerned with numerical minorities, as happened in the Great Society. In addition, other interests, either initially or after a while, may support aid for these groups, for example, the medical profession for Medicaid; the agricultural sector for food stamps; and the educational establishment, states, and cities for federal educational support. They may do so to further their own interests, those of the minorities, or both. In addition, if the votes of these minorities can make an important electoral difference, they may be appealed to by one or both parties, which can give them some leverage. The struggle now for the Latino vote is an example. On the other hand, the leverage of these minorities is often limited. One way to see this is in critical problems facing these people that haven't yet been solved where the government must play a crucial role if progress is to occur. Notwithstanding the various forces in play, the situation can be pretty bad for some in the society. If the majority doesn't care enough about this to commit the resources required to change the reality, democracy is of limited utility to these people.

The Consequences of Self-Love:
What Kinds of Problems Is Our Country Likely to Solve and Which Are We Unlikely to Solve?

The situation of numerical minorities who do pretty badly in our society, most notably in not getting the education that would give them opportunity to advance through their own efforts, shows the role of self-love or selfishness in affecting what happens, in this case the selfishness of a majority of Americans. That raises the question, what kinds of problems is our country likely to solve and which are we unlikely to solve in light of the self-love that predominates in our society? We are likely to find a way to deal with Social Security's fiscal problems, even if that involves accepting certain costs, because most people value, expect, and hope to draw on it. The same is true for Medicare. We are likely to find ways to deal with budget deficits because Wall Street and the business community are powerful, their success affects the prosperity of most of us, and they care about the deficit, especially over the long run. In contrast, we are far less likely to solve the problem of failing education for the poor and all that contributes to it because most people don't care enough to demand and support a solution, notwithstanding the difficulties and costs caused by these failures, and we do not punish politicians who fail to make significant progress in this area. The problem, as I have argued, is not with our politicians but with us. Self-love affects what we are able to do politically and what we are less likely to achieve. Politicians in a democracy cannot commit a massive amount of resources the people do not want to commit or will not support. This is even true in the area of foreign and defense policy though since World War II administrations have had more leeway in these areas than in domestic policy, but the great efforts of administrations to persuade the American people to back them in foreign and security policy show a concern with maintaining support. Our leaders are limited in their ability to persuade us to change who we are, what we believe and are willing to do. They are unlikely to try or, if they try, are unlikely to get elected, reelected, or be successful in leading us. Defense policy may be one area in which this general proposition does not apply. George W. Bush's doctrine of preventive or preemptive attack, its application to Iraq, and his efforts to gain the support of the American people represented a change in the country's foreign policy and an effort to change what the public would support in response to external dangers. Most likely, without the 9/11 attack on America, he would not have been able to do this. It is also worth noting that in doing this he did not seek a draft and also lowered our taxes so most people experienced little direct personal cost from the policy.

When one looks at leaders and what they can achieve, one sees the critical role the people play and the importance of our self-love in what our leaders can achieve.

Are We a Democracy?

In light of our discussion it is worth examining the question, are we a democracy? What does it mean to be a democracy? We use the word all the time, but its meaning is more multifaceted than we often realize. Democracy involves a variety of things, but we can begin our discussion by asking the following question. If the public does not demand that Congress pass significant campaign finance reform because they do not expect anything significantly helpful to be done, are we a democracy when that happens? Democracy doesn't require that the people demand campaign finance reform, but when they don't demand a change in our system, even though they are aware of the corroding effects of money on politics, *because they don't think their representatives will respond to their wishes by making truly significant changes,* then in an important way we are not democratic at that moment. Something is not happening that is supposed to happen. We can of course say the people need to be more insistent, more demanding, less easily discouraged, but they are who they are and in their action are not utilizing their democratic rights to gain what they want because they do not think their representatives will be responsive. This of course is a self-fulfilling prophecy. Absent public pressure, representatives are less likely to pass campaign finance reform that would remedy the problem of the influence of money. It is interesting that Congress finally passed campaign finance reform with the McCain-Feingold law, which despite its limitations did produce some significant changes though far from what was needed because of ways to get around it. The public did not mobilize to demand the passage of this bill, but enough representatives wanted it or feared the public's reaction if they voted wrong that they passed it. This shows the power of the public, especially when aided by motivated representatives, a power our public often doesn't seem to know it has and which it rarely uses. If the public insisted and held their representatives accountable, campaign finance reform, even more effective and with fewer loopholes than McCain-Feingold, would pass. In this case our system has democratic potential, which is important, but we are less of a democracy because that potential is not being used, especially on a matter as important as the role of money in politics. We should judge our democracy not only based on its democratic potential but also on the degree to which we utilize it. Some will say we do not have to use a right and can still have it, but if people don't use it because they think doing so would be useless, that right is in some important sense significantly lessened.

There are times when the public would not tolerate a failure to solve or resolve a problem. For example, if the United States experienced a severe recession or depression, the public would expect a change that would get us out of the severe slump. They would not accept their leaders and representatives not making changes that would alter their situation. In this area our democracy is stronger and more real in practice and effect than in the campaign finance case. Any assessment of our democracy would have to include these various realities as part of our account. How democratic we are seems to depend on what matters we are looking at. Of course, there is more to democracy than what we have focused on here, but we shall postpone that discussion for a while in order to create a basis for it.

Are There Limits on What We Can and Are Willing to Do Politically? Where Do They Come from and Are They Movable?

If Americans could get beyond self-love, a concern with themselves and their families that forgets or ignores the fates of others, they would be open to leaders who may have ways to solve certain problems. In solving our problems we are not confined in our means either to economic individualism (the market) or to democratic individualism in the form of welfare. We can, for example, improve opportunity. In trying to figure out what to do to solve certain problems, are there limits in how far we can go, limits to our action, because of self-love? Limits resulting from our self-love definitely exist. For example, most of the time Americans have qualms about employment policies creating public sector jobs, jobs the government creates and pays for. At the same time many workers and middle-class people do not have trouble with government created jobs in the defense industry, even on weapons systems the Pentagon says it no longer wants, or with government-created jobs that result from certain legislation, for example, environmental, disability, and agricultural legislation, but somehow paying poor people to clean streets and parks is considered in another category (except when we are in a Depression and people close to us are suffering and need jobs). We don't seem to believe in making sure that people make a living wage, have a reasonable standard of housing, medical care, and education. We seem to feel that if people lack some of these things, it is their responsibility or their family's. This of course reflects our culture, which emphasizes individualism and self-reliance and is partly based on self-love as well as a belief in markets.[13]

A critical question is whether these cultural and policy limits and constraints are movable. Can our culture or at least some of the beliefs we hold change, maybe with the help of politics and political leaders? When presented with this question as a general proposition, many may not want this change. The question, however, should be treated in specific terms and with specific examples, not generally, as that may affect the answer we give as to what we want. For example, if enough people find they can't afford healthcare, they may well want the government to provide it, even at the cost of higher taxes. Similarly, their attitude toward public sector jobs is likely to vary depending on how bad the economic situation is, how many are suffering, and especially whether people they know and those close to them have lost jobs and can't find new, adequate employment. Of course, in this latter case their views may depend on self-love rather than on moderating that quality. Equally important, there are times when what was not acceptable culturally becomes acceptable. For example, during the Great Depression welfare, which had been viewed pejoratively, became more acceptable, presumably because people you knew had lost their jobs. So too at that time, public sector jobs, such as the Civilian Conservation Corps, were accepted, even desired and gladly held. But as we emerged from the Depression, old attitudes returned. This illustrates the fact that in special circumstances cultural attitudes can change. Another example is emancipation from slavery, but that required a war and ultimately military victories to accept it.[14] Lincoln's leadership was important in that case, and he based his authority to issue the Emancipation Proclamation on his being Commander-in-Chief in time of war. FDR based his appeal for much of the New Deal by arguing that we needed to do certain things because our capitalist system and economic individualism, two fundaments of our belief system, had failed.[15] They were not providing people with the economic opportunity to provide themselves with basic necessities, and we needed to change that. Thus, Roosevelt used basic cultural ideas to deviate from what was culturally accepted, in this case by proposing and passing public sector jobs and welfare, among other things. So too Lincoln used basic cultural ideas from the Declaration of Independence, "We hold these Truths to be self-evident, that all Men are created equal, that they are endowed by their Creator with certain unalienable Rights, that among these are Life, Liberty, and the Pursuit of Happiness." He used these ideas to get Americans to abandon what many had culturally accepted, slavery.[16]

Can our cultural constraints be changed in more normal times? It is, of course, important that they can be changed in times of crisis, but can leaders in more normal times persuade us to support public sector jobs or laws that move us significantly closer to a living wage as well as some other necessities of life? This is much less likely if our self-love leads us not to care about the people who lack these things. It is also the case that global economic competition in a globalized world poses an additional problem here. Because of that competition, we may feel we cannot afford certain things. In the end our wealth, our productivity, *and* our values are likely to determine what we do. Neither the first two of these nor the third alone can do the job. All three are probably necessary. One could ask what we think we can afford to do now as the richest or one of the richest countries in the world, but the answer to that depends on our values and choices and gets us back to the problem of self-love. What after all are we willing to do for others besides ourselves and our families?

Are our leaders likely to try to enact such change and get us to accept it? History suggests they are not likely to try if they feel we will not support such efforts. One exception may be when they feel our security or existence is at stake. The few who do try to achieve this kind of change are not likely to be successful because such changes are often costly, materially benefit only a limited number of us, and thus do not win popular support. Even Lyndon Johnson tried to achieve only a small part of such an agenda and before long faced a reaction from people who thought he was doing too much for blacks. *The capacity of our political system seems to be sharply limited unless we the people change who we are,* and the ability of leaders to facilitate this change also seems limited in normal times. It is true that in wartime we ask the people to make sacrifices, which they do, but usually when the war is over Americans have wanted to end the sacrifices as soon as possible and get on with "normal life." In sum *our political system cannot be much better than we are.*

What Kind of Democracy Are We?

As we have seen, our democracy affects what problems we can solve. Democracy here means much of what we ordinarily mean, competitive elections, republican government, free speech, association, petition, press, and so on. As we have suggested, it is unlikely we will be able to solve some of the most important problems we have if the people do not support doing so and do not support the substantial commitment of resources required. For example, to make our worst schools work probably requires not only substantial additional funding for the schools, but also changes in the communities where they exist starting with the creation of jobs, a difficult and expensive task in many of these communities. This is why self-love *and* compassion are critical in affecting what happens and critical to the study of politics. Because of who we are, and we are typical, not exceptional in our nature, and because we are a democracy, we often leave the least fortunate among us in the lurch.

Many contemporary democracies are social democratic with significantly higher taxes and a larger role for government than in the United States; in fact, most advanced industrialized democracies are that way, for example, most countries in Western Europe and Canada, but America will not become social democratic without the support of our people. Many Americans seem not to want to become a social democracy. They like the fact that their taxes are lower than Europe's, and they fear big government and what some call "socialism." Helping the least of us have a reasonable standard of living, however, does not require the social democracy Europe has, but we are reluctant to do it.

While our democracy has certain failures, it has provided us with many benefits and should not be abandoned. The question we have focused on is whether we can solve some of our most important unresolved problems and, if so, what it will take to do so. One cannot discuss our democratic challenges without recognizing the importance of the 9/11 attack on America and what it means for our priorities. We are currently preoccupied with fighting terrorism, as we should be, and that limits how much we can do on other fronts. Even if we were not so occupied, it is unlikely we would make much progress on some of our most important unresolved problems.

The public and government reaction to 9/11 will also create and pose democratic challenges. Initially the people didn't know what to do, but wanted terrorism handled so they trusted President Bush and supported him. By the time negative, even catastrophic consequences occur as the result of our attack on Iraq, if they occur, and by the time great negative public reaction occurs toward government policy, it could be in one sense too late, for example, when one of our major cities is catastrophically attacked. The people at that time can say they want a different policy and set of leaders, but that will happen too late to have prevented the negative consequences.

Democratically the most that could have occurred before the war with Iraq was a congressional debate and public discussion on what should be done, a debate that in principle could have said no in one form or another or have delayed the attack, while trying to get more international support. In fact Congress and the general public did not say no. Our democracy can also be assessed by asking whether the questions that should have been raised and considered were. In fact, the debate in Congress about going to war with Iraq was very limited. The serious opposition to the war at the elite level was also quite limited. Senator Byrd was an exception. Senator Kennedy spoke on the matter as did former Vice President Gore. Former President Clinton raised serious questions early on and then became quiet. Apparently a number of potential critics decided it was their obligation not to repeatedly question the president's policy once he made clear his intentions. Going to war was Bush's call. It was inconceivable Congress would limit military action by refusing to appropriate money for the troops once they were there. Congress may with great difficulty be able to limit appropriations marginally and incrementally over time, but even this is uncertain. It was inconceivable Congress would not authorize the war, once Bush made his intentions known. To do that would have raised questions in the world, in the view of many representatives, about American foreign policy and America's role in the world and would have undermined the president's negotiating position. The irony is our war with Iraq has raised these very questions. If the war in Iraq and its aftermath come to be viewed as a large mistake, that might change Congress's stance in the future about such matters. If that happens, the president and Congress may be more circumspect about what they take on.

In the debate and discussion prior to the Iraq war the most that could be achieved, besides seeking, gaining, and mobilizing support for the administration position, would have been the raising of critical questions. Some questions were raised, especially about what we would do in Iraq once Sadaam had been defeated, but they didn't seem to make much difference in what happened. More important, the significance of going to war with Iraq and its effect on future terrorism and the War on Terrorism were not sufficiently addressed, especially by critics in Congress who questioned the war and got media coverage. The significance of preemptive or preventive war as a doctrine we were implementing and its possible future effects on international relations and on us were not addressed much by critics of the war in a way that received major news coverage. These were major and important failures of our democracy because much was at stake in the decision to attack Iraq. This matter was sufficiently important to the future of America and the world that these momentous questions should have been raised, even if the outcome would have been the same, which was likely.

Was there any way our democracy could have worked better here? Only if representatives had more courage in presenting, pushing, and even regularly repeating their questions, reservations, and issues. Those questioning representatives would have to believe the country could survive strong debate and even a close vote and still continue its central position in the world, a position that reflects our power, and still aggressively wage a war on terrorism. It is likely the case that had the Congress not authorized the war, it would have had profound effects on American foreign policy and the perception of us in the world. Nevertheless, all things considered, the questions raised by the

Iraq war were too important not to be the subject of much more discussion by our representatives.

What is the significance of our problems, both those we have reasonably resolved and those we have not, for the future of our democracy? Clearly the quality and worth of our social, economic, and political system are affected by how we do for the poorest and most deprived of us. It is also affected by what we do for the rest of us, especially the vast middle class. Generally we have done reasonably well for the middle class including a significant part of the working class, though now it seems to take two income earners to support a family, with consequences for child care. Recently our middle class has been threatened by the outsourcing of jobs to other countries, and this problem is very much on their minds. The fact that our country has the double task and ongoing responsibility of serving the masses as well as the most deprived and disadvantaged of us makes matters more difficult and challenging because the former task often occupies our attention and energy. For example, our government worries a lot about the state of our economy, because that affects how most of us fare, and in the new global economy because of increased competition as well as increased opportunity, such a focus is important. Nevertheless, in the short and probably the longer run these two areas compete for resources along with our defense and security needs.

What costs do we pay because our system doesn't work for certain people? We have crime, areas of our cities we will not go in, welfare, less productive and unemployed workers, a drug trade, and so forth. These are definite costs we pay as is the moral cost of being a less worthy country and being less worthy ourselves, but we have become accustomed to them and have adjusted to them. It's almost as if we consider them the "cost of being who we are" in our society. If we get too bothered by crime, we simply create harsher penalties and build more prisons, at least until that gets ridiculously expensive. When we get disgusted with welfare, we pass welfare reform that limits how long anyone can be on welfare and what work they need to do to get it. It's as if we don't think much can be done to alleviate this whole set of problems and we accept them, probably so we can get on with our own lives. As long as these problems don't touch us directly, we go on with our lives and focus little on them and what it will take to solve them. We simply do not think much about the most disadvantaged in our society. This is a selfishness that results from a self-love that ignores the situation of others. Most of us are hardly touched because of these problems, and we are the majority. Thus, our country remains stuck as far as resolving these problems. *This is a problem of democracy dominated by self-love, and it is our problem.*

Madison in the *Federalist* No. 10 foresaw that self-love would be a problem for democracy, one it would have to deal with in some way.[17] However, he limited his focus on the problem because he was more interested in preventing government action than in facilitating it in order to solve certain problems.

Because we accept the disadvantages of others as "part of life," and may even convince ourselves, if we think about the problem at all, that those who are disadvantaged could change their situation for themselves or at least for their children if they wanted to badly enough, we do not insist these problems be solved or reduced significantly, as evident in our actions, which speak louder than words. In that way we continue to be our lesser selves and to have a less worthy society and political system. Madison's major way of dealing with self-love, which tried to block factional action in government, doesn't help us because what is needed to alleviate these problems is governmental action, not its blockage.

If Morality Is Critical for Solving Our Problems, What Is the Role of Religion?

It seems obvious that many of the problems we face require our morality if we are going to resolve them. If morality is critical for solving these problems, both at the citizen and officeholder level, it is reasonable to ask what role religion will play in affecting that morality. In raising this question, I do not assume religion is the only thing that affects morality, but it plays an important role. James Madison did not expect much from morality or religion in dealing with the problem of self-love.[18] Consequently he focused on creating a political system where faction would counter faction so that majority factions, which he defined as adverse to individual rights and the aggregate interests of the community, would be hard to form, where ambition would counter ambition, and power check power. America has certainly benefited from these arrangements in important ways, but clearly has not solved all its most important problems. What is needed now seems to require the compassion that morality and religion sometimes facilitate and build on, *a compassion that involves not only concern but action that follows that concern*. It is interesting that secular humanism and religion each criticize the other on the same grounds, that they fail to create moral citizens whose morality and compassion we can benefit from. As we know, getting us to love our neighbors as ourselves is not easy. In any case, we must acknowledge that under Madison's system we in America have not solved all our critical problems.

George Washington believed we needed religion to make our system work.[19] Nevertheless, constitutionally we subscribe to the separation of church and state, as so many of our Founders thought desirable. To quote, the first amendment says, "Congress shall make no law respecting an establishment of religion, or prohibiting the free exercise thereof. . . ." That does not mean religion has no role in American society and in the choices we make, far from it, but the role is not a formal one, established by law. Clearly, religion has not made us so compassionate or moral that we attend to the problems described here in a serious, sufficient, and sufficiently committed way, the way we attend to our own affairs and those of our family. While leaders from time to time can appeal to our better selves, "the better angels of our nature" in Lincoln's words, it is doubtful they will be able to turn us around by themselves. *What they can achieve depends on our morality and compassion.* Our skeptical, cynical selves, of course, often do not seem to take their appeals seriously, regarding them as rhetorical flourishes, which distances us from our responsibilities. Religion, morality, and compassion as they exist in most people now will not solve the problems posed in this book nor are they panaceas that by themselves will solve all our most important problems, but morality, compassion, and religion developed in us could be enormously helpful. Each of these faces its own challenges in helping us change our practice. Nevertheless, each is relevant, so relevant that it merits careful attention as part of the study of politics and society. In fact, each probably deserves central attention if we are interested in solving our most important unresolved problems. Later in this work we shall have more to say about this.

What Can Be Done?

If we suffer from a shortage of morality and compassion, what is to be done? Is there an appeal that will be successful? What if there isn't? If an appeal that will help us solve our seemingly unsolvable problems doesn't exist, what does one do? Legislatively you pass and governmentally you do what you can. You try to keep the economy strong to help as many as possible, recognizing there may be tradeoffs between economic efficiency and distributional justice, you encourage charity, and you push for Democratic or Republican programs and victories or for a third party, depending on your view of what will be most helpful.[20] These are some of the most common actions people pursue. All these make sense as alternatives, in light of the status quo, but none of them change it significantly when it comes to dealing with some of our most fundamental problems. Most progress in America, when it occurs, is incremental and sometimes suffers setbacks. *All of these efforts together, unfortunately, are probably not enough to get the job done, which is why we cannot avoid the role of morality and compassion in dealing with our most important problems, both in this country and in the world.* We will have more to say about this at the end of this work.

Why Focus on Particular Problems?

In assessing the American political system how have we decided which problems to focus on? Americans face many problems and challenges, some more important than others. For example, a healthy economy is important and affects what we do on other fronts. Some of our problems are more easily solved than others though few of them are easily resolved. We have argued that we are likely to deal with and somehow resolve the financial problems of Social Security and Medicare through some mix of remedies because these are such popular programs in which many citizens feel they have a stake. Other very important problems are much less certain of resolution. The example we have used is failing education for many students in our least successful schools. This problem is very important and has figured predominantly throughout this book. America has a significant segment of its people who do not have the skills and training to make them employable and able to earn a living wage. Since particular racial or ethnic groups are overrepresented in this unemployed and underemployed group, this is even more of a problem, and if this continues from one generation to the next, which has been happening, it is an even greater problem. We have discussed the consequences of these failures, unemployment, welfare dependency, crime, a drug trade, illegitimacy, teenage pregnancy, single-parent households, and the like. Most important, *the problem of failed education touches the heart of our beliefs.* We believe in individual opportunity to better one's situation, it is a core belief, and we know that education and the discipline that goes with it are critical to this. That is why we favor a good public education for all, including the poorest and most disadvantaged among us. We mouth these words and in some way believe them. We just have not been willing to face and make the commitment this belief requires. Because successful education is often critical in affecting the quality of individuals' lives and a yet to be achieved goal for many, it is a central problem facing and testing America. This problem has served and will serve as a prism for assessing critical aspects of American politics because it is central to our core beliefs and represents what is a major failure, perhaps the major failure, in America. Some, of course, will say that almost all Americans have opportunity and that those who fail educationally are just not using it. When one sees how few students in these failed educational settings manage to succeed, one has to question that conclusion. The fact that only a few are successful, rather than showing that opportunity exists for most, as is often argued, shows rather that real opportunity exists for only a few. When one realizes that education, like most worthwhile ventures, depends on faith, in this case the faith that being successful in school will lead to a good job and a good living, and realizes what kids see in poor neighborhoods and towns with so many unemployed and those employed barely making a living, one begins to understand why so few succeed. When one realizes that the quality of education does not depend alone on what happens within the school building, but also depends on the community where that school is located and what is happening there, one also sees why this problem exists. Unfortunately, saying that these kids are the victims of low expectations and then having higher expectations of them, without doing what it will take to help them achieve those higher expectations, will not get the job done.

Of course, one should also evaluate our political system by looking at the middle class, but in this work we focus primarily on failed education, mainly affecting the poor, because that so violates our core beliefs about opportunity. A focus on the poor could also include the issues of employment, jobs that pay a living wage, housing, child care, healthcare, and crime, for example, but the primary focus here is on failed education. The analysis of why we fail in the area of education also applies to our failures in these other areas. In evaluating our political system, one could look at issues that affect all classes, and some issues just listed do that, and also include issues involving the economy, the environment, how we live, political participation, and the role of America in the world. Again, our focus is more sharply defined here with the primary focus on failing education as it affects the most disadvantaged. Our ability to deal with this problem as well as with others is affected by the attitudes of the American people, including our skepticism and cynicism toward politics. We turn next to that topic.

Why Is the American Public Skeptical and Cynical?

We have pointed out how cynicism and the skepticism of the American public affect our politics in important ways, and we must ask why the American public is cynical and skeptical. These qualities are most likely multiply determined. Our cynicism is tied to the perceived and real influence of money on politics, particularly in the form of campaign contributions. When citizens in a poll say they don't expect the government to do the right thing all or most of the time, a measure of trust in the government, they are likely responding to the influence of money, among other things. The peoples' skepticism toward government probably reflects something else as well. Whatever the reality, and government does a lot that is positive and that citizens take for granted and don't even think about, most Americans expect government to do little for them during most of their lives. Most think that much of what happens to them is a result of their own efforts and perhaps some luck, and they are encouraged to believe in the importance of their own efforts by our culture's focus on freedom, individualism, and self-reliance. Citizens seem to be able to distinguish what government can and cannot do. To mention just two examples, steelworkers want tariffs on imported steel, farmers want agricultural subsidies. There are a large number of these special cases, but in general most citizens expect government to have a limited effect on their lives and personal economic success. They do expect the government to help make the economy strong and usually hold the president and his party responsible if the economy weakens. Their self-love, manifested in their desire to do well economically, leads them to certain expectations of the government. Nevertheless, our expectations of government are limited, compared for example to what occurs in many European countries and Canada. These limited expectations are tied in with our society's conception of limited government and its skepticism and sometimes distrust of government. Most other advanced industrialized democracies do not have these same views, as seen in their social democratic governments, which tax, spend, and do more, with their people's consent. So part of our skepticism of government, both as to what it needs to do and can do, is culturally based and comes from our view that government can solve only certain problems and do only certain things effectively, and in many areas cannot do as well as we can individually in our private lives.

These generally held public views reflecting skepticism and cynicism are partly justified. The way in which they are justified will be apparent to many. How these views are partly unjustified may be less apparent. Sometimes Congress and the president, for example, do not follow the mobilized moneyed interests. This happened to a significant extent in the Tax Reform Bill of 1986.[21] Similarly, the president and Congress sometimes do what is in the public interest on matters of public importance, including occasions when doing the public interest requires actions that are not popular. Deficit reduction in 1990, 1993, and 1997 are examples as was the Social Security reform of 1983 and the gradual deregulation of energy prices passed in the late 1970s and early 1980s.[22] There are numerous other examples such as the passage of Medicaid, the Children's Health Insurance Program, and other programs. It is doubtful majorities demanded these. Thus Congress has on various occasions passed sometimes liberal, sometimes conservative legislation in the public interest. Most people haven't perceived this and haven't thought about it. So Congress and the president and, for that matter, our citizenry sometimes merit cynicism and skepticism, sometimes not. However justified or not, these attitudes do exist, and it is important to recognize their effects. Above all, they discourage paying much attention to politics and participating in it, justify a quite limited involvement, and encourage us to focus on satisfying our own needs and wants in the private sector. Media coverage of our politics and our leaders reinforce and reflect these tendencies, a topic to which we now turn.

The Public and Media Coverage of Politics and Our Leaders

Sometimes our people are disaffected with their leaders. We make jokes about them. We say they are not very bright or articulate (George W. Bush, especially before 9/11), have character flaws (Clinton), are not articulate and lack vision (George H.W. Bush), are not smart and are oblivious to parts of reality (Reagan), are ineffective (Carter), paranoid (Nixon), untrustworthy (Johnson), and so forth. Most of the time we don't expect a great deal from them, even in the beginning of their terms. The attack on America on September 11th changed that for a time as we recognized the seriousness of the attack and the dangers posed by terrorists, quite possibly grave dangers. When we recognize the country is in deep trouble, an example was the popular response to FDR in the Depression, the people often support the leader, at least initially.

On the other hand, those who track presidents closely in normal times, as they are covered in the news, often see a focus on the "soap opera of the presidency." One can see this with most any president. Here are some examples. Will the president be able to work with an almost evenly divided Senate, will he be able to pass a particular piece of legislation he has made his highest priority, how will he deal with his differences with other countries, will he be able to pass a voucher system tied to his education bill, will he get his way on patients' bill of rights legislation, if he doesn't, will he veto, if he vetoes, how will Congress respond, will he get his way on Social Security reform, and so forth? Is he up or down in the polls, more or less influential with the Congress, can he and will he recover, what do his reelection prospects look like, how will his approval rating affect his party, and so forth? All these can be important policy and political questions, but they can be and are often treated in ways that smack of soap opera, especially by the cable news networks. Does that mean the public follows the president in the same way? Apparently certain media outlets have concluded this kind of coverage attracts more viewers, which means politics is being followed in this way by these viewers.

By way of comparison, it is worth looking at the coverage presented in the aftermath of 9/11. Because the dangers were more serious, the coverage was less trivial. Drama did not have to be created; it was there for everyone to see. War with Afghanistan, then Iraq, made the drama more real and extended it.

Since the soap opera mode is so frequent, what should we make of this? Clearly it is an effort to create some drama, even in the form of melodrama, to entertain. In the judgment of the media, presumably based on market research, without this highlighted drama the president, politics, and policy are not sufficiently entertaining or interesting. This of course is a self-reinforcing process since one has to get into a subject to see its interest and Americans rarely achieve that. As long as coverage is superficial, tastes are superficial and vice versa. What is the significance of this for our politics and political system? It certainly reflects and reinforces ignorance and lack of understanding, and also responds to a lack of interest. The lack of interest comes from the fact that government decisions are rarely seen as decisively affecting one's life and that most people don't see a payoff from following politics closely.

The primary news media for most Americans is television. As commercial enterprises, most networks give people what they want in news coverage in order to get good television ratings. Much coverage of the major issues of politics and policy is superficial. Networks are often looking for brief sound bites from politicians. Apparently the networks have decided this limited coverage is what most viewers want. A number of the cable television networks, which cater to a more specialized and limited audience, often substitute heated if superficial argument for light in the mini-debates and disputes they present.

Why do most citizens, as revealed in their behavior, not want deeper news coverage? Apparently most of the time citizens are not that interested in learning much about the issues their representatives face. Either they think these decisions won't affect them much or they believe that whatever views they personally come to hold will not affect what happens. The latter view is corrosive in a democracy and also serves as a rationalization for their limited involvement. Citizens simply are not interested in policy in any depth most of the time. On the other hand, citizen interest in what to do after 9/11 and what the attack meant for the future was an interesting and important exception for a limited period of time, probably because Americans could see that the world of politics could affect their lives in a major way. *For too brief a period they glimpsed the truth.*

What interests citizens in news coverage? Apparently the drama, even the melodrama, and conflict. While the conflict and drama can be relevant, the details of what politicians are fighting for and about are given less play and short shrift. It's the conflict that gets the coverage. Almost as soon as one election is over, literally within days, sometimes within hours, discussion turns to the next election, who the likely contenders will be, and so forth. *It's too much the drama and too little the substance of politics*, the issues and the policies. The drama becomes the substance because politics and government are entertainment. We view politicians as seeking their own welfare and power, rarely as seeking policies and wanting power to affect policies. Seeing them as self-serving makes for a reality that is easier to comprehend. They do of course compete for power, but often they do so to stand for and carry out certain ideas. This is part of what is often left out or shortchanged in television and newspaper coverage. Apparently we don't want to put much into our political participation, even as spectators. It is not enough to realize that. We must ask why. That may be one of the most important questions of all.

Most of us do not feel a personal need to participate in politics other than as superficial spectators most of the time, probably because we get or think we get most of the benefits we focus on from the private sector, not government, partly a result of our capitalist system. We also believe we should gain most of our benefits through our personal efforts, not government, and we expect most of the important benefits we get from government to continue, whether we pay close attention to politics or not. So why participate? This is a result of our culture and what we have been taught by experience and otherwise. Most of us believe that our deeper and stronger political participation will not make much difference to what happens including what happens to us. All this affects both our participation as actors and spectators in politics and affects how the media covers it. *The consequence is a less empowered citizenry exposed to a more superficial politics.* What we do not see and what too many of us forget, if we ever knew it, is that politics can greatly affect us, our future, and that of our children and grandchildren. The question is, will we see this in time?

Partisan Conflict and Its Effects on Citizens

One cause of citizens' skepticism and cynicism toward politics results from what many Americans perceive as the sniping partisanship of our parties. Many Americans do not seem to understand nor have much tolerance for conflict, which is at the heart of politics, whether that conflict is about goals, means, or both. They see how each party tries to embarrass or blame the other, but don't see that this can help the public evaluate the contending parties if it can respond to these evaluations critically. People seem to object to negative ads, even as they are influenced by them, and seem not to understand that the act of criticism is legitimate in politics and policy and of potential use to citizens. It is possible that many citizens don't trust their own ability to evaluate these various claims, and one response to this may be to say that neither party can be trusted. At the same time, many voters identify with one of the parties and vote that way. Most likely the people just want the government and officeholders to take care of things, that is, resolve the conflicts and do the right thing, and so are uncomfortable with mutual attacks by the parties. They don't want politics; they want solutions. But somehow that misses the point since politics is about conflict, conflict over what we should do and how we should do it. It is also possible that this reaction to partisan conflict is just one more basis for criticizing government to justify the critic's non-involvement.

How Our Not Being More Involved Politically Limits Us

We have seen the limited political involvement of most Americans. Only about 50 percent of eligible citizens vote in presidential elections and only 35 percent participate in off-year congressional elections. Most Americans have fairly limited knowledge about politics, have even less knowledge about policy, and most participate very infrequently. One way to understand this limited involvement is to ask why people participate in politics. What does an individual perceive she needs and wants from government that would motivate her involvement? Much of what people want from the government, for example Social Security and Medicare, they already are entitled to under the law. As we have suggested, many things we want we get through the private sector or think we do. On the other hand, if we think about it, there are a lot of things for which we depend on government, for example, roads, being able to deduct the interest on our home mortgages, food safety, drug safety, disease control, security, and many, many other things. We take for granted many of these services until there is a problem with their provision.

The government is also critical to what we want for others, for example, adequate public education. Through my private efforts, if I am a member of the middle class, I can try to increase the chances of a good public education for my children, for example, by making enough money to be able to live in a community that has good school systems, but I cannot do that for poor kids. I need the government to help achieve that. If people say, "why can't the poor get a good education for their own children," the answer is fairly obvious. They would if they were in a position to do that. So for some goals we depend more on government than for others. Of course, if people as they live their lives are not much interested in the fate and welfare of others, they may require less of government as far as helping the disadvantaged.

Because we do not have the social democracy many advanced industrial democracies have, we are not so dependent on government for benefits and services, and we look to it for less. This is a self-reinforcing process. On the other hand, over time we, including the powerful and numerous middle class, have come to depend on government more. Prescription health benefits for Medicare recipients are a recent example of this. A population that looks to government for benefits and services is more attentive and more participant. One sees this in the elderly who feel a great investment in what happens to Social Security and Medicare.

Our interest in and expectations of government also depend on our culture. Is it a problem that most Americans seek most of their goals through the private sector? No. In fact, it is probably generally more effective and efficient to operate that way. Most Americans are doing pretty well but we do have the problem of those who are not. Is it a problem that most Americans because of our culture and the way we live do not pay close attention to politics? For many purposes no. However, one place a problem does occur is for those people whom the private sector is not serving well, in particular, the poor.

Significance of Nonvoting

In our political system a large percentage of our citizens don't vote. Apparently the nonvoters do not think voting is worth their time, energy, and effort. It is of course true that the poor and less educated vote less. They may well feel the system isn't doing much for them or that their vote will not change anything. On the other hand, lots of poor and less educated people depend quite a bit on government for certain programs and who wins elections would likely make some difference in their lives. Most likely, they do not believe they could make a difference in affecting what happens, but given their numbers they are mistaken. This is true for the non-poor as well.

Nonvoting reflects alienation from the process and the system. Nonvoters do not see themselves playing an active part in the political process and do not feel empowered. Many of them see little reason to follow politics and be informed and they are unlikely to join with others to promote their common purposes. Some suggest these people don't vote because the political agenda doesn't grab them. An agenda that might grab them, if they believed it, would probably involve a substantial redistribution of resources, which of course is an agenda that could turn off many middle-class people so politicians have to be careful how they appeal to these nonvoters. This of course gets us back to one of our major themes, the importance of self-love and selfishness in the political system, especially as it affects the middle class and others better off than the middle class. For the most disadvantaged to be concerned about their own situation and to want to better it seems reasonable, especially if they are quite disadvantaged and barely making it or perhaps not making it. For those who are comfortable to exclusively focus on their own situation, to want to better it and not worsen it materially, and not to care about the situation of the more disadvantaged is more selfish.

Since Government and the Private Sector Do So Much for Us, We Feel Little Need to Be Active Politically

Politically we are isolated from each other. We rarely work together for political purposes. Much of what we want we get from the private sector through our own efforts, from our jobs and the income they produce. Much else that we need and want is funded by our taxes and done by the government, whether federal, state, or local. Our sense of what we can expect from the government is also affected by what the government has done and is doing for us. Since many of our wants are satisfied through the private and public sector, notwithstanding our complaints about government, we may conclude there is little reason to get involved locally or at any level of government. If we are getting about what we expect to get, why do we need to get involved? Many Americans act accordingly. In the social democracies of Europe where taxes are higher and government does more, citizens participate more because they have higher expectations and are more dependent on the government, for example, when they are dissatisfied with their national health programs or by a reduction of government subsidies of higher education.

Should It Bother Us That Politically We Are So Isolated from Each Other?

Should it bother us that politically we are isolated from each other? What are the costs of this, both now and in the future? When the time comes when we want to mobilize politically, and one promise of democracy is that we can mobilize when we want to, will we be less able to do so because we have little experience with that? Perhaps it will take more for us to get moving politically because it is not a habit, we are out of practice, but it is extremely unlikely we have lost our capacity to mobilize. On the other hand, when we do mobilize because we feel things are very, very wrong, will we be more vulnerable to demagogic politics, a politics based on emotion and simplification, because of what has been our shallow involvement in politics. It is interesting to ask whether those who already are somewhat knowledgable about politics and more involved in it are less vulnerable to demagogic politics. It seems as if some, probably a minority of those who are more involved now, are also vulnerable to this, and democracy will always be threatened by the potential of such politics. Perhaps the best defense against the dangers of demagogic politics is political discourse involving openness, reflection, and people with a variety of points of view, but most Americans just don't see the need or have the desire to do this, and that is unlikely to change. That is one of the reasons why our Founders came up with a system of checks and balances and sought other ways to limit majorities including the Bill of Rights.

Many people want to limit their political involvement and want to spend their time doing other things. This, of course, is their right. The right not to be involved much in politics is one of our freedoms. Consequently, we have to create a viable political system that takes into account this desire to limit one's involvement in politics, and we have done so. As we have argued, there are inevitable costs that follow from this.

If the government is a second power system intended to protect the less strong, and that is an important function of government, will it be harder to grab the attention of people politically because of their noninvolvement? Probably, but even more important, it is likely to be easier to manipulate them, including demagogically, because of their lack of knowledge. Germany in the early 1930s is an example of a people so manipulated as they tried to escape from a period of great economic hardship. It is striking and a bit surprising we haven't had more demagogic politics. We have short sound bites, which simplify and sometimes play on emotion. Demagogic politics occurs more often on some cable networks and some talk radio. What constitutes demagogic politics is of course a judgment that the listener or observer must make. Is each party's criticism of the other party demagogic? Probably. Do they counter each other? Often, but whether most partisan followers are listening, open to, and thoughtful about these counter claims, which themselves may be demagogic, is questionable. Perhaps we have been fortunate in that the demagoguery we have had hasn't led to the disasters that occurred in Germany with terrible consequences for the world.

For the most part politically we are spectators, often superficial ones at that. Sometimes as spectators the public can determine what happens politically, at least as far as general direction, but often in normal, ordinary, day-to-day politics the viewing public does not determine what happens in policy. The void the public creates is partly filled by money, and the influence of money in politics encourages skepticism, cynicism, and noninvolvement in the public, which paves the way for the continuing influence of money.

Do People Need to Be Involved in Politics?

Do people need to be involved in politics and, if so, what kind of involvement is necessary? To become informed in order to vote doesn't require that much, especially if you have cue givers you trust. Mobilizing politically requires more effort. The involvement that is most important is paying close enough attention to politics that you have a sense of some of the most important issues and know enough about them to decide your position reasonably, that you vote, that you sometimes make your views known to officeholders and not just by voting, that you sometimes talk to your friends and neighbors, and that sometimes you join with others to achieve something politically when you think what is at stake is important enough. People need to know enough to decide reasonably because often they will be appealed to demagogically, by an overly simple and emotional appeal, and some knowledge may give them some protection against this though limited knowledge does not always protect one from demagoguery. Are people who watch and read political news as diversion or entertainment "involved"? They are in a certain way, but how valuable that involvement is to their being responsible citizens is open to question. It likely depends very much on the purposes of those who provide that diversion and entertainment.

It doesn't seem to bother most Americans that we are not that active politically. It should bother us if there are key problems that are not being rectified because of our lack of political involvement. One area where public involvement really might improve things is in the area of campaign finance and the influence of money. Because the American people are alienated from their political process, as seen in their cynicism and skepticism, they are vulnerable to demagogic manipulation in this area. For example, a common argument put forth by politicians opposed to the public financing of campaigns, probably the most effective way of dealing with the problem of the influence of money, is "I don't think taxpayer money should pay for the campaigns of politicians like me." The public's noninvolvement, lack of thought about the significance of campaign finance, and skepticism makes them receptive to that argument. What they don't think about is they pay heavily now because of the influence of money, and public financing of elections could reduce that influence.

Whether greater political involvement would reduce public alienation is uncertain. That would depend on whether people felt they made any progress as a result of their efforts. Most citizens simply do not want to spend their time on such efforts. Given the frequent slowness of the democratic process, it is unlikely that will change.[23] In democracy perhaps what is most important is that citizens, when they are moved to get involved, can and, if enough do so, can change things. Of course, sometimes the people's involvement may come too late to avoid suffering for themselves and others.

Does Lack of Public Participation and Discourse Mean Representatives Are Not Fundamentally Accountable?

We have seen that public participation and political discourse among Americans are limited. People may occasionally talk with their friends about some important matters, often with people with whom they expect to agree, but more typically little talk occurs even on major issues, and even the talk about presidential candidates may be very abbreviated and public participation very limited. However, this does not mean our representatives are unaccountable. If the people don't like the state of the country or their own situation, they can vote incumbents out of office. Because most people are inactive, they often do not know specific actions of their representative or senator of which they would disapprove. Consequently, they are generally not likely to hold their representatives accountable for specific actions. But that does not mean their representatives are unaccountable. Citizens in effect decide what they pay attention to and what they will ignore though their skepticism and cynicism may discourage them and also justify inattentiveness. On the other hand, politicians, political parties, and interest groups often have incentives to flag certain issues, positions, and actions. These may or may not grab peoples' attention, but those who flag these issues are trying to do this and often choose their criticisms accordingly, for example, by voicing complaints they believe people will respond positively to.

Some might argue that because of the people's inactivity and inattentiveness, representatives are basically unaccountable, but in an important sense this is mistaken. Accountability means representatives can be held to account for what they have done, what the government has done, or for the state of the country. People have the capacity to hold representatives accountable whether they use it at particular moments or not. Accountability is important because it can be used, and representatives know that. The people by their actions determine when and how they will use their power. In the past when things have gotten bad, they have used their power to replace incumbents, the Depression being an obvious example. On the other hand, it is also true that representatives often are not held accountable for particular actions they have taken because the people don't use the power they have and don't take the time and effort required to hold their representatives accountable.

The people often do not know their own power. One can see evidence of that when representatives fear to vote against their interests in particular circumstances. For example, in 1986 the final votes for the tax reform bill reflected the fear representatives had that if they voted for special interests, they might be punished. This same fear is seen in Congress reversing itself on catastrophic medical care legislation in the late 1980s and also on the issue of withholding taxes on interest from savings accounts in the early 1980s. Representatives try to anticipate public reaction to what they do, which keeps them "honest" to some extent, particularly when their actions cannot be kept invisible. All of this suggests that despite the limits in public participation and discourse in America, representatives can be held accountable and know that. How accountable they are depends both on us and on them. Needless to say, representatives prefer having some leeway for a variety of reasons, some meritorious, some not, and how much leeway they have also depends on them and us.

Patron-Client Relations in America

As we look at political systems, democratic and otherwise, around the world, we see the importance of patron-client relations. A patron supplies rewards of various kinds to his clients in return for their loyalty. Often this has been viewed as a more primitive form of democracy and politics. To what extent do patron-client relations occur in America, what is their significance, and to what extent and in what way does our politics move beyond that, even if it includes some elements of it? Most Americans are not dependent on political patrons for their jobs. They receive various benefits because of legislation, for example, Social Security, and do not have to depend on individual patrons to supply those benefits. At the beginning of the twentieth century progressives tried to reduce the frequency of patron-client relations through civil service reform. Nevertheless, we should not be surprised to see patronage and patron-client relations in our politics. It may be that when people lack the education they need to get jobs in the market or when the supply of workers outnumbers the demand for them, patronage becomes more important. People with less education and income may depend on this more because they are in a weaker position in the market. Politicians have long understood that the more they do for people, the more loyalty and support they are likely to receive. For example, Franklin Roosevelt understood this from his New York experience and his experience in the Depression. That is what his advisors meant by "tax, tax, tax; elect, elect, elect." Needless to say, certain businesses that want tax breaks, subsidies, regulatory exclusions, or help from government will develop patron-client relations with government officials and those seeking political office.

Does it make sense to think of certain national programs, for example Medicare, as involving patron-client relations? Ordinarily we don't consider Medicare an example of this since it is a program that by law everyone over sixty-five is entitled to. Medicare benefits are not a favor to a particular person who then owes loyalty to the particular individual providing the favor. A category of people benefit whether they support particular politicians or not. On the other hand, the elderly often support politicians who back Medicare, and both parties have learned to do this to gain backing. Because support of parties and candidates does depend on their views and actions involving Medicare, there is an aspect of patron-client relations involved, but it is different from the way these relations are usually conceived. Another example would be the oil industry, which gets special tax breaks and supports politicians who push and pass these with campaign contributions. We have a tendency to see more primitive forms of patron-client relations, for example, the exchange of jobs for political support in old city political machines, as a less advanced politics and a less advanced democracy than we have, but this analysis suggests we have similar or related phenomena going on, even in our "more advanced democracy," though we may sometimes try to avoid the most primitive versions.[24] The fact that a whole category of people benefits from Medicare means it is not just a benefit for a particular individual that depends on the good will of a particular patron. Because so many benefit from it, a group is empowered, currently thirty-five million elderly, rather than an individual who is alone in his relation with his patron or one of a few.

In our political system we want people not just to care about what is good for them individually or for their group. We also want them to be concerned with what is good for their community, the public, the society, the country, and the world. Lots of people do think about what is good for themselves and feel legitimate in doing this because they think what is good for them, their family, and their group is in the public interest. A problem occurs when this is our exclusive focus. Concern about a politics involving patron-client relations reflects the desire that we not just care about what's good for our particular group and for us. To the extent we widen our concern, we will have a more advanced politics and democracy. Even though we have a politics that limits patron-client relations, we still face the problem of too exclusively caring about what's good for us and our group and excluding to too great an extent a focus on what's good for others, for the whole society, and for the public interest.

Broader Collective Aims and the Public Interest

Many political scientists are reluctant to speak about the public interest, partly because they believe people will not agree as to what it is. Rather, they choose to speak about "broader collective aims" or some similar concept. This concept of course begs a number of questions, such as whose collective aims, just as in using the concept of public interest one has to face certain questions. But we must ask whether there is an important difference in which language we use. Usually when we speak of the public interest, we are speaking of it as we perceive it. "Broader collective aims" suggests what some "we" are striving for, what we or others believe are worth striving for. But the words "public interest" suggest there is a public interest, a true public interest. One always has to acknowledge that we may or may not understand the public interest correctly, but those who use the concept believe a public interest exists. What has driven people, especially scholars, away from the concept, public interest, and made them reluctant to use it? The awareness that people differ on what it is, and justify all sorts of things in its name, led to the view that it should not be made the basis of a political science that strove for objectivity and an empirical, scientific approach not dependent on people's values and subjective views.

Clearly if people came to believe that their broader collective aims would actually hurt society, they probably would not seek them. So whether we use the term public interest or broader collective aims, we presume people know what they are doing or think they do and act accordingly. The problem with eliminating the concept public interest from our analysis is that without it, how can we focus on our not dealing with certain problems and how can we select which problems to focus on? We identify particular problems we are not dealing with because we think they concern matters that are part of the public interest, even critical to it, and that they therefore merit our attention. We need a concept of the public interest in order to be critical, to evaluate what our country is and is not doing. If we do not have such a concept, we could find ourselves in an absurd situation. For example, many Germans shared a number of important collective aims articulated by Hitler, for example, getting the economy going again, getting out from under severe war reparations, and so forth. Yet the aims Hitler pursued and the way he pursued them brought destruction and devastation to Germany as well as many other horrendous results. We have to be able to say, as do ordinary German citizens, that the set of broad collective aims Hitler sought for the German people and the way he sought them were a great mistake. We have to be able to do something similar in America or in any other political system and in the world. Citizens feel free to do this all the time as do politicians. The study of politics is not served by avoiding this language.

Political science generally has avoided the concept of public interest because scholars sought a status different from politicians and ideologues. Many hoped to gain objective knowledge independent of their point of view including instrumental knowledge, for example, what is needed to produce something and what are its consequences. But to describe politics without evaluating it, without a critical stance, is often to miss the significance of what is being described. Since politics involves evaluation, such a stance suggests that political science has little or nothing to say about this decisive sphere.[25] Does this mean that what is being described and its perceived importance may depend on one's view of the public interest? Absolutely. Does this mean that political scientists may have to defend their views of the public interest at times? Yes, but so what? Even now when some students of politics try to avoid the term public interest, any careful and thoughtful reader can and will evaluate both the significance of what has been found and its nature. This is a proper part of the study of politics, and it applies as much to us as to our readers.

One response by political science to this dilemma has been to focus on instrumental relations, what leads to what, what has what consequences, with political scientists suggesting that how you evaluate the goal to be attained, the means to do so, and its consequences depends on your values. Notwithstanding this position, which can be useful, one needs to recognize that the study of politics is concerned with values, with what is valuable and what is to be avoided. Even deciding what is important to study often is aided by a sense of values and a sense of what is worth examining and evaluating. Each political scientist must work out for himself what is valuable.

We also should avoid relativism, the belief that every person's evaluation is as good as everyone else's. We have to be able to make judgments about various notions of the public interest and evaluate various claims, both as individual citizens and as a collective. This is critical to our assessment of the political system. The public interest is an important part of what politics should be and is about. Politics should not just be about what's in it for me. Clearly our evaluations and judgments will depend on our values and principles, which themselves are based on judgments. It is inadequate to say your values are yours, mine are mine, and our judgments are tied to them. We must be able to contest them as well as allow them to contest in the public arena for that is the stuff of politics.

How does language affect whether and how we deal with the issues discussed above? If we use terms like "broader collective aims" or "diffuse goals" to describe the goals either of the public or officeholders, we will be missing part of the point. It is part of our job to assess how the political system is doing and to do that we, whether as individual citizens or students of politics, have to have a sense of what is worth doing, what is valuable. How else can we assess the importance of what we have failed to achieve or, for that matter, what we have achieved? This is obvious to most citizens, but it is not embodied in the language of most political scientists though sometimes we have hidden our own views and values in the language of "broader collective aims."

How Good Is Our Conception of Our Self-Interest and the Public Interest?

We assume in our political arrangements that people think about and know their own interests, especially their self-interest, and sometimes we assume people will think about the public interest. It is not hard to show that people often not only do not know what is in their own self-interest, but often have a distorted view of the public interest.

People's interests are affected by poverty and racism, to take two examples, whether they realize it or not. Money is spent to fight crime, lock people up, pay welfare. People without skills are often less productive, in the material way we measure productivity and if they can't find employment and don't pay taxes, that leaves us with less materially. Crime makes us afraid to go to certain places at certain times. There are beautiful parts of the places many of us live that we would enjoy more were we not afraid of crime. The less skilled people are because of failures of education, the less productive they are likely to be, which affects how the rest of us live. Despite all this, we rarely think about how we are adversely affected by poverty and racism. We accept the consequences of poverty and racism almost as a given. We have become accustomed to these costs. We learn where we can go and when, we move away from crime areas if we can, we pay for police in the cities and sub-urbs to protect us, and we become accustomed to the taxes we pay, including for police and prisons. We focus on how we can improve our own situation through our own private efforts and ignore the situation of others, especially if they don't live where we do. We seem to accept these negative conse-quences in our environment and adjust to them, much as we accept and ad-just to the weather. Only if our lives are suddenly sharply affected do we be-gin to notice what is going on. Most of the time our lives are not sharply affected. Thus in some important way we don't see how our material inter-ests, let alone our other human interests, are adversely affected by poverty and racism, even if we are middle class and not members of a group that suf-fers racism. Of course, reducing poverty and the negative consequences of racism in our country would cost money, certainly in the short and interme-diate term. Maybe Americans know this and choose to live with the status quo. They may not believe significant benefits would come from such an in-vestment or maybe they just do not want to pay the price themselves in higher taxes.

In these cases either we don't think of the common good or, if we do, we think of people mostly like us, in our situation or class, and don't think much about those who have the least and are much worse off. Somehow we don't include them in considering the common good, if we think about it at all, or we discount, disregard, or ignore them, intentionally or without thought.

There are of course people who pay higher, more obvious costs because of poverty and racism, for example, those who live nearer to poor areas and who can't afford to move. If we don't live where they live, we don't experience these costs nor do we experience the costs paid by the poor and those who suffer racism. We may know cognitively or intellectually that the poor and the victims of discrimination suffer, but we don't experience those costs, and that makes all the difference. Furthermore, we don't want to know and don't want to think about this.

We are incapable of knowing the public interest because our view is too limited, cognitively, analytically, and experientially. If we don't know our own interest or know only part of it and don't know the public interest or only know part of it, how do we function in a political system that is based on the notion that we will pursue our interests (our happiness). We can of course say, as we do, that people are pursuing their interests as they see them. Maybe we speak this way to avoid having to face the fact that we pursue chimera, false Gods.[26] We have values and things we value, and we need to be critical in choosing what these are, whether we are or not. If we are mak-ing great mistakes in the pursuit of our interests, maybe the truth will catch up with us, but not necessarily. The more powerful we are, the more we have been able to fend off some negative consequences of our mistakes, the less likely we are to see the truth, in time. One reason people used violence against America may have been to communicate that we have made mistakes or omissions, as they saw things. To see that is not to justify this violence, but to explain at least part of what motivated them.

We value and take pride in our freedom, the freedom to do what we want, pursue what we want, pursue happiness, but if we are pursuing some of the wrong things, our freedom may be less valuable. Are we slaves to certain conceptions of what we want even as we think we are free? We may be. It is not surprising that some other advanced industrial democratic countries consider healthcare, education, a job, and some minimum income aspects of freedom. What they see as freedom is part of freedom just as what we see, for example, free speech, association, press, and elections, is part of freedom. How do we make sure we are working on both fronts? If we are not aware we have a problem, we are less likely to do this. In fact, we are not aware of the ways in which our freedom is real, but limited.

Notes

1. Jonathan Kozol, *The Shame of the Nation* (New York: Crown Publishers, 2005), 281.

2. To give a sense of the challenge we face, ". . . in cities like Washington, D.C. the school system fails despite spending more money per pupil than world-class public schools in neighboring suburbs." Juan Williams, *Enough* (New York: Crown Publishers, 2006), 98. The difference in achievement is not surprising when one thinks of all the educational supports kids in these wealthy suburbs get even before they start school, compared with the experience of poor children. Williams also points out ". . . a 2002 study showed that 65% of big-city school districts, which have the highest minority populations, is higher than the average per-pupil spending in the rest of their state." I point out it is likely to cost more to educate students from disadvantaged backgrounds. Smaller classes, educational aides to teachers, and tutors are needed. The state figures Williams cites also include poor rural districts, which have similar educational problems. A lack of hope and faith is a problem poor students face, which Williams recognizes and wants to rectify. I absolutely agree with him that black families, I would add poor families, have the power to improve the education of their children "by turning off TV, by demanding good grades, and by going into the classroom to work with teachers." Overseeing homework would also help as would a restoration of hope and faith in the kids. All this is needed, as is the allocation of greater resources to poor schools and the communities that house them. Success will require the efforts and resources of the poor and the non-poor, of minorities and whites. The racial and

class segregation in our schools, which Williams points out, 98–99, also make educational success for the poor more difficult to achieve. Only the efforts of the poor and non-poor, minorities and whites, can change failure to success. If and when that success is attained, it will be one of the notable achievements in our history.

3. Sometimes our representatives and leaders, with or without our help, solve important problems. The comments here refer to large problems we are unable to solve such as the failures of our educational system. Each of us could identify other large problems we have not solved, but in this book I shall focus mainly on the problem of education.

4. E. E. Schattschneider, *The Semisovereign People* (New York: Holt, Rinehart, and Winston, 1960), 40–41.

5. Schattschneider, *Semisovereign People*, 37–41.

6. Schattschneider, *Semisovereign People*.

7. Jeffrey H. Birnbaum and Alan S. Murray, *Showdown at Gucci Gulch: Lawmakers, Lobbyists, and the Unlikely Triumph of Tax Reform* (New York: Vintage, 1987), 285.

8. James MacGregor Burns, *The Lion and the Fox* (New York: Harper & Row, 1975), 274–75.

9. Robert Dallek, *Flawed Giant: Lyndon Johnson and His Times* (New York: Oxford University Press, 1998), 168–69.

10. Haynes Johnson and David S. Broder, *The System* (Boston: Little, Brown, 1996), 11–12.

11. Erich Fromm, *Escape from Freedom* (New York: Avon Books, 1941).

12. Robert Putnam, *Bowling Alone* (New York: Simon and Schuster, 2000), discusses this lack of social trust and cooperative civic action in a variety of ways.

13. If a business feels it needs subsidies to increase its profit or even to be profitable, it will seek them if it believes it has a reasonable prospect of success, notwithstanding its belief in self-reliance and markets.

14. James M. McPherson, *Battle Cry of Freedom* (New York: Random House, 1988).

15. Burns, *Lion and the Fox*, 274.

16. Gary Wills, *Lincoln at Gettysburg* (New York: Simon & Schuster, 1992).

17. Alexander Hamilton, James Madison, and John Jay, *The Federalist Papers* (New York: New American Library, 1961), 78.

18. Hamilton, Madison, and Jay, *Federalist Papers*, 81.

19. George Washington, Farewell Address. In John C. Fitzpatrick, ed., *Writings of George Washington*, Volume 35 (New York: Greenwood Press), 229.

20. Part of your moral obligation, whether you recognize it or not, is not just to care about yourself and your family, but also to be open to and face the facts as to what would be most helpful to different parts of the society including those who are disadvantaged.

21. Birnbaum and Murray, *Showdown*.

22. Sidney Waldman, "How Congress Does the Difficult," *PS: Political Science and Politics* XXXIII, no. 4 (December, 2000).

23. Putnam, *Bowling Alone*, discusses the problem of civic involvement more generally.

24. Robert D. Putnam, *Making Democracy Work* (Princeton, NJ: Princeton University Press, 1993), discusses these various forms of political involvement.

25. The author is grateful to Wilson Carey McWilliams for pointing this out.

26. Perhaps one reason some people are attracted to religion is that they sense they may be pursuing false Gods. Maybe that is also why some say truth and values are relative, that is, relative to our views, both as recognition of what is going on, but also to escape responsibility, as when they say "that is who I am and what I believe" without really examining their beliefs critically.

~

CHAPTER FIVE

Is There a Role for Morality and Religion in Our Political System?

The Role of Morality and Religion in Controlling Self-Love

As we saw earlier, one of the country's founders, James Madison, believed that morality and religious motives could not be counted on to control self-love, what we would call selfishness, and the way in which, to use his language, passions affect opinions.[1] Because of the problems self-love can lead to, Madison focused on a number of ways to limit majority tyranny. His purpose was to prevent certain actions, and with the benefit of history we see he had notable but not complete success. Madison notwithstanding, sometimes what needs to be done requires positive action, not simply preventing action, and here Madison's ideas are inadequate. To get the people to do certain things, for example, to support what it will take to make our schools work, requires moral or religious motives and their lack can pose problems. Needless to say, religion doesn't always play a positive role nor are moral considerations free from error and distortion. The fact that morality and religion have both sometimes been misused and abused or have had limited positive impact does not mean they are not useful, even necessary, to solve certain social problems. They are in fact critical.

It is, of course, true that members of the elite, for example, those who hold office, can contribute to the solution of problems without being pushed by the people, but the greater the redistribution and transfer of resources required to solve problems, the harder it is for the elite to pull this off, even if they want to. Of course, if they have the support of Wall Street and the business community, as they had in the 1990s with deficit reduction and in the late 1970s with energy pricing to increase production and decrease consumption, that can propel and allow action, but not all problems are of sufficient interest to the business community to do this, for example, failing education in certain areas in America.

This means we cannot dispense with the need for morality in our political affairs, as Madison attempted to do in *Federalist* No. 10. We need it. To the extent that we do not have it, we will be revealed in our shortcomings, as we are.

The Lack of Compassion and the Moral Limits of Our Political System

Because of the importance of compassion, which involves for our purposes action and not just feeling for the suffering of another, and the importance of its lack in political and social life, it is something we need to take seriously and study. We need to figure out what causes and allows it, in what circumstances, what its limits are, and how it works.[2] While Rousseau, Marx, and Rawls, to mention just three political theorists, focused on the problem of getting people to care about each other, there is much more work to do. Compassion and its lack are quite critical to politics as is self-love, and they merit our attention. While such matters are often viewed as the concern of idealists, they have great practical consequence, both in their presence and absence.

We have been looking at some limits of our democracy, especially its moral limits. We say we believe in opportunity, but many, perhaps most of us know that for some opportunity is really quite limited. We just accept that fact. Sometimes to make ourselves feel better we think that those who don't make it aren't smart enough, motivated enough, or hard working enough. We don't know them, and most of us have never been in their shoes so we can believe whatever we want. It seems obvious, when only a small minority make it out of the most disadvantaged backgrounds, that opportunity is in some important way lacking. Partly to make us feel better, our political leaders often say and do things that suggest they are making a serious effort to improve the situation of the disadvantaged, implying that they and we care, but lots of times these efforts are quite inadequate, demand little of us, and lead to little if any improvement. Most of the time we just don't think about the lack of fundamental opportunities as long as we and those close to us have those opportunities.

Freedom and Morality

We have raised moral questions about the way we function in our political system. We now need to ask how our focus on freedom as a central feature of our political arrangements relates to the question of morality. How do we see freedom today? Most of us think it means doing whatever we wish, as long as it is within the law. We see it as taking advantage of our opportunities. We expect people to seek their own interests, and we do not describe most of our behavior as selfish and self-loving. We don't consider being captive to our wants and desires to be a form of enslavement. We don't have a concept of moral or civil freedom such as that described by John Winthrop over 300 years ago.

> Nor would I have you to mistake in the point of your own liberty. There is a liberty of corrupt nature, which is affected both by men and beasts, to do what they list; and this liberty is inconsistent with authority, impatient of all restraint; by this liberty, Sumus Omnes Deteriores (we are inferior); 'tis the grand enemy of truth and peace, and all the ordinances of God are bent against it. But there is a civil, a moral, a federal liberty, which is the proper end and object of authority; it is a liberty for that only which is just and good; for this liberty you are to stand with the hazard of your very lives.[3]

Winthrop's concept is as true, probably more true and valuable, when the authority he mentions is a moral authority that comes from within us as individuals. Freedom is not just doing whatever you wish, without restraint, especially your own restraint of yourself. Otherwise we are inferior, not what we can be and were meant to be. To do whatever we wish, without restraint, can be an enemy of the truly valuable and of peace. There is another freedom, a freedom we rarely talk about, to act morally in a just and good way. This is the highest and most valuable freedom. If we are told what to do and it doesn't come from us, that is not the freedom we should aspire to. If it comes from us and serves our wants and desires without regard for others, including the most disadvantaged among us, whether in this country or the world, that is not the most valuable freedom and not what we should aspire to. We are meant for more than that.

In recent years we have seen a period of moral relativism in which each person is seen to have his or her own morality, and no one can persuasively claim that one view is better than another. We say our collective purpose is to allow everyone to be what he can be, whatever that is, and most of us believe that. However, many of us do not fully appreciate the moral implications of this when it comes to providing real opportunity to others. When you combine our moral relativism with our stress on opportunity, as we practice these, the result is that most of us seek what we want without thinking much about others beyond our families and loved ones. At the same time many of us are religious, both in what we believe and in our church-synagogue-mosque-going habits. Is that because we see something missing in our lives, which leads some of us to religion and keeps us there? Yet if religion were successful, we would not have the problem of self-love and selfishness we have. Clearly many who are religious, but do mostly what they want, with limited moral constraint, are making limited moral use of their religion, whatever else they are achieving through their religious connection. Of course, many secular humanists are also concerned about seeking a more meaningful, moral life, but it's not clear they are doing any better than those who are religious.

If we do not see or seek the moral freedom Tocqueville, Winthrop, and others have described, how can we see the limitations of our society and lives? Our conception of freedom is radically limited and we understand only part of what freedom is. Realizing this is an important step for every generation.

On the Lack of Discourse and Reflection in Our Political System

On most of the most important questions we face in our lives no one can persuasively claim exclusive knowledge. We have a need for discourse and reflection, but unfortunately these rarely occur in the public. Instead on television we sometimes see representatives of different positions, one of whom simply claims x is clearly in the public interest while the other claims it is not. Rarely do they really engage each other, really speak to and with each other. Lots of times they ignore what the other has said, do not come to grips with it, and make whatever points they wish to make, disregarding what the other has said. Politicians often do the same. This produces the conflict TV likes, but it does not produce the conversation and reflection that could be helpful to the viewing audience. Whether the internet can help us move beyond political segregation to help fill this void remains to be seen.

How often do political discourse and conversation occur among the people? Usually we speak about political matters with those who agree with us and, if we disagree about something we see as important, we often avoid the topic. One way we deal with disagreements is to say you have your opinion, I have mine, and that lets us off the hook as far as discussing and pursuing things. We are making our "individual" decisions, and we do not ordinarily treat them as subjects to contend over. If the subject is very contentious and important to us, our focus can turn to who is with me, who is against me, and, most important, who will prevail politically and how can my side win. Much in politics then becomes instrumental and is perceived that way, for example, what move is someone making to win the argument or the election or the policy decision. The focus also is often on who's prevailing, who's likely to, whom do they have to win over to succeed, what obstacles might they face, and so forth. Politics also becomes deal making. What has to be done to create a majority coalition or, for that matter, to block a majority? The problem is not that politics occurs in these ways since that is part of democracy; rather, it is that the discourse that should be part of politics too often does not occur, especially in the public, but also in the media.

Is the lack of discourse problematic? We believe in free speech, it is a fundamental premise of our system, but what is being said, what is its nature, and who's listening? Most of us do not appear to miss the discourse. Real political conversation takes time and effort, and most of the time we don't want to expend these. We'd rather spend our time doing other things. It is doubtful if the quality of our discourse changed, many would be pulled in. The commercial media, particularly television, have clearly made a judgment that we are not interested in real conversation since they generally present something quite different. What is lost because of the absence of real discourse in our political system?

Democratic politics involves our deciding what we wish to do. It presumes our speaking, but are we listening to each other? As we speak, are we even assuming others are listening and not just those who already agree with us? Politics of course can be a quick assessment without much deliberation of where we stand followed by a decision, often by majority vote. If there is no discourse, no speaking *and* listening, we are missing out. We are not taking full advantage of free speech, which we so value.

Affecting Our Own Outcomes: The Surprising Role of Morality

One reason we limit our political involvement is that often we do not believe our political actions will affect our outcomes. This reveals a blindness in us since if enough of us act, it can affect our outcomes.[4] However, for us to act to gain what the economists refer to as public goods, selective incentives are needed.[5] These are rewards a person gets only if he acts to gain the public good. Many things we seek and desire are public goods. These are goods whose benefit one gets whether one contributed to the gaining of the good or not. Peace, the benefits of victory over the Nazis in World War II, a clean environment, and good roads are a few examples of public goods, as the economists define that term. To act to gain such public goods voluntarily, without coercion, an individual has to receive some benefit contingent on his contribution to the gaining of the public good. Otherwise, he lacks an incentive to contribute and if enough people do not contribute to the gaining of the public good, it will not be achieved, often to the detriment of most people. What has been rarely seen is that morality can help solve this problem if it is widespread enough because it provides the selective benefits needed for action to occur.[6] If people feel rewarded when they do what they see as the right thing, they will be motivated to act and their outcomes will change, first because they will get the psychological benefit or pleasure of acting morally, second, because if enough people are so motivated to act, the actors may provide the public good that also provides benefits.[7]

To recapitulate, if because of our moral views we believe certain actions are good, if we do them, we get a reward, i.e., we feel better about ourselves. If we don't act, we do not get that reward and may even feel bad because we did not act. Thus morality can get us to act and, because of that, is extraordinarily important in politics and, for that matter, all social life. Of course, we have to believe the act is worth doing. For some this means the act will make a difference in achieving some goal besides our moral satisfaction. That is why cynicism and skepticism about politics are so paralyzing, enervating, and disempowering. If people believe a certain action, even a moral one, will produce no positive result, most probably they will see no reason to do it. In those circumstances to act, one has to believe that a given moral action is good in itself, worth doing in itself.[8]

Because moral action can be rewarding in itself, even if it produces no other benefit, political and civic action can change a person's outcomes, even if it produces no other change. Since in life one often tries to effect change and make a difference without immediately accomplishing that, this is a useful incentive, especially since change may eventually occur as others act.

Some argue that the motivation to act morally because it gives one pleasure is selfish. But that motivation, which has to appeal to our moral sensibility to work, may be one of the most powerful forces causing people to act morally. To focus on the pleasure the act brings the actor is to beg the question whether the action is valuable beyond the pleasure it brings you. What is important is whether the act is valuable in itself, valuable as an example to others, and valuable for what it produces. Needless to say, much turns on the moral sensibility and judgment of the actor. It is not enough to think your action is moral. What is most important is whether it is moral. People have done awful things in the name of morality, which alerts us to the importance of the question, is what someone believes to be moral really moral? We cannot escape this question and the responsibility that goes with answering it. To say that someone acted morally because of the pleasure of so doing and that therefore the action was selfish is to miss the importance of moral action and to demean it. That does not mean the pleasure one gets from acting morally is not important. It is very important because it often motivates moral action. People utilizing their democratic rights and taking advantage of their freedom to act may depend on such a motivation. Once one recognizes the importance of the motivation to act morally because it gives one pleasure, one sees the importance of morality and moral sensibility in affecting the politics, society, and economics of a place. Much turns on that morality and moral sensibility. While such concerns have often been labeled idealistic, they have great practical import as they greatly affect the quality of our social and political life.

The fact that different people have different views of morality does not reduce its importance nor does it alter the reality that the quality of our country and world depend on our morality and moral sensibility. In the end each of us has to make his or her own moral judgments. While laws can help, people make the laws so they also reflect our moral sensibility. The alternative to individual responsibility is for an elite to make these judgments for us, and that is undesirable and dangerous. Who will guard the Guardians? Despite the fact that there are disagreements about what is moral, we cannot avoid relying on our morality and compassion if we are to make a better world.

How Shall We Evaluate Our Political System?

How shall we evaluate our political system to see how we are doing? There are many criteria we could use and it is doubtful there is one criterion that should be the exclusive basis of our evaluation. One way to evaluate our political system is to see how well we do in resolving certain important and critical problems in the country since that is one of the tasks of governing.

Another way to evaluate our political system is to see what the most powerful person in the country, the president, can do to help us solve our most important problems. Much of the time we evaluate presidents as they deal with ordinary and typical problems, such as proposing and trying to pass a budget, dealing with national security in normal times, and dealing with the issues they have chosen to focus on, often ones they have spoken about in their campaigns. As we have seen, in ordinary times, but even more when great issues confront the country, the president is the one who poses fundamental questions about policy and the polity.[9] Who are we? What do we believe and stand for? In light of that what do we need to do? The president decides when these questions need to be posed and is in a position to gain attention when he does so. Lincoln did this before and during the Civil War including in the Gettysburg Address. Franklin Roosevelt did it during the Depression and also once World War II started. Presidents sometimes must do this to help solve certain problems and to close the distance between presidential weakness and presidential aspiration in certain situations where the president must move the public and Congress.[10]

Once we understand the critical role of the president as leader *and* see the limits in what he can do, we will be in a better position to evaluate our political system. We should also evaluate our political system in terms of our core beliefs. Perhaps our most central core belief focuses on individual freedom, a freedom that allows us to take advantage of opportunity, to try to make of our life what we wish. The inalienable rights of our Declaration of Independence are life, liberty, and the pursuit of happiness, the liberty to pursue happiness however we see that, as long as we don't deny others their rights or break the law. Clearly education affects our ability to make use of opportunities and our freedom, so the failure of our educational system for many, many poor and disadvantaged is a stain on our country and on us.

In a classic statement Erwin Hargrove says to achieve the deepest aspirations of our culture, the leader has to engage in transformational politics by evoking such aspirations "in a manner that tells the truth about the practical steps needed to fulfill them." President George W. Bush attempted to evoke such an aspiration when he spoke of leaving no child behind, but clearly neither he nor any other politician has been able to get Americans to make the commitment to education required. This is not just a weakness in Bush. It is a weakness in our politics and our political leaders in modern times. Since most money for education comes from state and local taxes and education is mainly controlled by state and local government, the states determining what powers local governments have, we see the failure at all levels of government. Pointing out how failed education limits freedom and opportunity has not changed the reality. Some people of course say no one is denying these kids education. If they want it, the argument goes, it is there for them. In light of the number of failures in our worst school systems, and there are a huge number of them, and the small proportion of students that succeed, one might think such people would know better, but they don't. This is a failure of understanding that no leader has been able to rectify. Evoking our deepest aspiration, for freedom to pursue opportunity, just hasn't convinced the American people to make the commitments needed to drastically reduce our educational failures. It is of course true that to really transform things, one has to understand and present the practical steps needed to fulfill these aspirations. Lyndon Johnson's approach, like Franklin Roosevelt's, was trial and error, but you need enough support to begin the trials and sustain them. Rectifying our educational system where it is failing requires too large a commitment of resources to "sneak" reform through. There is no chance the reform of No Child Left Behind will achieve the transformation sought. Perhaps Americans know that, which is what limits their interest in the enterprise, or perhaps most of us just don't care very much. Our national commitment is limited because politicians know Americans don't favor a greater commitment. For political reasons we cannot do what must be done to solve this problem. This suggests our real aspirations may be different from what we say they are. Most likely what concerns us most is freedom and opportunity for ourselves and our family rather than for others in America. As long as people like us have good education and the freedom and opportunity to use it, we're satisfied. *In some important and fundamental way we do not see the others*, those who are denied basic educational opportunity. If our actual aspirations are as described here, these others are out of luck.

It may be the American people do not believe the No Child Left Behind policy will create successful education. If so, they are probably correct. But they would not support what would achieve this since they don't care enough to pay the price. Again this suggests true educational opportunity for all is not among the deepest aspirations of our culture. Americans may believe certain groups and individuals aren't doing their part to take advantage of their opportunities, but life teaches most of us, if we pay attention, that people need hope and faith to put in the work to take advantage of opportunities, faith their efforts will pay off, and, for many who come from disadvantaged backgrounds, these are lacking because of what they see around them. If we really cared about these people and educational opportunity for all, we would ask what we could do to help nourish that hope and faith. Politicians seeking office are unlikely to speak these truths because most Americans don't want to hear them, probably because a great redistribution of resources would be required to fix the problem of failing education. If some politicians have the courage to try, they are unlikely to win support because most Americans don't care enough.[11]

Erwin Hargrove, as we saw earlier, suggests that leaders who would appeal to popular majorities must discern and evoke unresolved problems and suggest plausible remedies that reinterpret shared beliefs and values in new, appropriate ways.[12] Most of our leaders have perceived the unresolved problem of failing education, but have they been able to "evoke the problem"? What do those words really mean? You have to get the public to see, really see, and care about the problem enough to support what is required to solve it. That our leaders have been unable to achieve. This is not primarily a problem of rhetoric, finding the right words. The people have to be open to your words, ready to take them in, and we have not been. We, at least a considerable majority of us, have a failure of compassion. The easiest way to see this is to compare the attitude of two different people toward those who lack health insurance and healthcare. One has a seriously ill family member who lacks health insurance and the other has no seriously ill family member and has health insurance for his family. The first is much more likely to understand the need for universal healthcare than the second. Another way to understand the importance of an absence of compassion is to compare the attitudes toward welfare for people during the Depression with the attitudes of those living in normal economic times. In the 1930s with 25 percent of the people unemployed and a very large number seriously affected by the Depression, people realized they could be hit by this and their attitudes toward welfare changed. In both cases some people see, really see, suffering that is not due to personal weakness, but more saw this when the Depression hit or when a family member was seriously ill without health insurance and that experience made all the difference. This is not just a matter of perception, which is why the concept of really seeing is used here. People can cognitively know there is a problem in our educational system, most do, but they need more than that to support the changes required. Perhaps one can capture this difference by contrasting experiential and cognitive knowledge. Sometimes one has to have knowledge in the gut to want to do something about a problem. If so, that is unfortunate since most of the time we lack that knowledge. It is very difficult for a president to evoke a problem we don't really see, and it is very unlikely he can make us see it. Most of us do not have experiential knowledge of failed education, where you don't feel able to do what you are expected to do, don't want to face the significance of your inability, and the class is constantly being disrupted by unruly students including you. The lack of this knowledge is an enormous problem for American politics because it limits what we do. Of course, this doesn't only apply to education; it applies to other important matters, often problems affecting the disadvantaged but not only them.

Because no president can evoke the problem of failing education in a way that will get to most citizens, none can suggest substantive remedies that will solve it which are also politically doable. This is because the necessary remedies require a large commitment of resources the public will not accept.

What is most likely required is a redistribution of state funds from the better to the worse schools, an increase in federal expenditure, and an increase in state and federal taxes to fund poor schools, both urban and rural. It likely costs substantially more to educate a poor, underperforming child in a poor school than it does to educate a child in a good, successful suburban school, even though the latter almost always has substantially more per student funding. Not surprisingly parents of kids in good schools want to give their own children every opportunity and, as a general rule, do not want to take resources from their own kids' education to pay for the education of other less achieving, more problematic kids. It is also far from clear how much in additional taxes they would support to deal with failed education, but probably their support would be limited. Once one begins to have a sense of the necessary changes that need to be made outside school buildings to improve the communities where these failing schools exist, the costs become even greater, probably substantially greater, and harder to gain support for. If the president and other political leaders cannot evoke the problem, they will not suggest the needed remedies because they know the public will not support them. Political leaders may well support some changes that do not require lots of resources such as vouchers, regular testing, and even some private tutors for kids who are failing. Some of these changes may help marginally, but they will fall far from getting the job done.

Political leaders sometimes evoke problems in a superficial way, even as they appeal to our beliefs and values, but offer reforms that will achieve little. No Child Left Behind is an example. The appeal and suggested solutions are superficial and the results produced do little, which only contributes to public skepticism about solving the problem. Basically our beliefs and values as they apply to individual opportunity for certain others are weak and have not made us feel we must solve this problem of failed education. The charade that results reinforces our skepticism and cynicism and, since we do not want to blame ourselves even though we are the critical ones in limiting what is done, we blame politicians, principals, teachers, bureaucrats, and the primary victims of these failures, the poor. The problem lies not with these others but with us the people. These others will be critical in solving the problem, if it is ever solved, but they cannot do it without our support of a *very* large reallocation of resources, possibly one as great or greater than what we spend on defense.

This example illustrates what is often the case. While it is not difficult to identify what is required for presidential leadership, for the president to lead successfully is another story. The heart of the problem is that most of us do not really see certain realities, our imagination is limited, and political leaders cannot make us see them. *Our difficulty is the problem of compassion and its lack. We cannot put ourselves in the shoes of certain others, and this limits our moral capacity.* If these were our kids who were failing and we were a numerical majority, we would do everything we could to turn around their experience. As a majority, we probably could change the politics of education and thus change education. Because the parents of kids in failing schools are a numerical minority nationally as well as in the states, where control of most educational resources ultimately rests, what they can achieve politically is limited. Again the problem is not with our political leaders; it is with us. Because of us, our leaders and representatives are limited in what they can do, and our country is the worse for it. In an important and fundamental way we are less of a democracy as a consequence. In pointing to our own complicity in this problem, I do not mean to suggest it can be solved by our efforts alone. Without the help of students, their families, and their communities we cannot solve these problems, but without the government and our help they cannot solve them alone. Both are needed.

A "leader who commands compelling causes" has great personal influence over followers.[13] One can see this in the immediate aftermath of the 9/11 attacks on the United States. The American people were very supportive of President Bush's response to those attacks, including against the Taliban rulers in Afghanistan and Al Qaeda. The support continued when Bush proposed and then launched war and regime change in Iraq. The American people wanted to be taken care of, wanted to feel and be safe, wanted the president and the government to protect them, and wanted to believe the president was doing that so there was initial support for Bush and the policies he pursued. The reality Americans experience after the period of this initial support will affect his support and most probably support for his party.

To more fully understand the possibilities of and limits on leadership, and the relevance of our morality to that, we need to look at American culture and the possibilities of cultural leadership.

Cultural Leadership, Culture, and Morality

One of the central tasks of political leadership is cultural interpretation.[14] This leadership describes what we aspire to and is often presented to us as who we are, that is, what we believe in and care about. Most presidents speak in these terms regularly, for example, in Inauguration and State of the Union speeches, but usually as listeners we don't pay much attention to this, dismissing it as rhetoric. This dismissal usually means the president hasn't gotten through to us on this level, which is the usual state of affairs. When he does get through, we take the words seriously and find them meaningful. For example, when President Bush said we do not do what terrorists do, intentionally kill civilians, it is likely we heard that and did not consider it window dressing.

Because political leadership is cultural interpretation, we need to look at American political culture since it provides resources for leaders as well as constraints on them. A traditional way of describing American culture is to focus on our emphasis on individualism, especially economic individualism, and the market, but also to recognize our desire to rectify some of the inequalities caused by the market.[15] I find it more useful, because it better describes what is going on, to focus on self-love as the central element in our culture and, as a less strong but real theme in our society, the need to correct for this, at least to some extent. Self-love should not necessarily be thought of as bad. However, if it is the only thing that motivates us, that is excessive and wrong. Different religious traditions have tried to capture this in different ways. For example, from the Talmud, "If I am not for myself, who will be for me? If not now, when? If I am only for myself, what am I?"[16] Similar ideas can be seen in other religious traditions, for example, love (care for, take care of) others as you love (care for, take care of) yourself, do unto others as you would have them do unto you, and do not do to others what you would not have them do to you. Most people would have a difficult time meeting the first two standards in the previous sentence, and the last one is also not easy to meet.

Self-love usually includes the desire to do well for your family as well as yourself and is not bad in itself if it is not one's exclusive and excessive focus. We sometimes recognize and act on the need to balance and correct for self-love, but often we don't. *Both self-love and whether we can balance it greatly affect democratic government.*

One faces the question, how much to balance self-love with a concern for others and how this can be done. Adopting the golden rule as well as the standard, do not do to others what you would not have them do to you, still requires morality and moral imagination since you have to be clear about what you would not want done and what you would want done to yourself in various situations. Applying these standards, for example, to what educational opportunity you would want for yourself or your children in different social situations might show the difficulty of translating these standards into specifics. Further, one requires compassion and imagination to follow these guidelines since you have to be able to imagine what it would be like if what was being done to others was being done to you. Needless to say, this imagination and compassion are often lacking. Offering general guidelines to help people figure out how to balance self-love with an acted upon concern for others does not necessarily make decisions easy, even if people wanted to show such a concern, which often is not the case. There is no way to avoid the fact that we will have to be moral and compassionate and make appropriate choices if we are to balance our self-love in the way we should.[17] One problem is that it is too easy to say I am concerned about others, not just myself and my family, and yet do very little about it. That is what most of us commonly do.

The way our culture affects our democracy can be seen in its effects on the leadership we have in our political system. Democratic leadership involves helping us solve problems when we need help. Sometimes, often on large matters, this means moving the public or at least getting them to accept what their leaders and representatives propose to do and are doing. Lyndon Johnson's Great Society including his War on Poverty is an interesting example because the public accepted what he did, at least initially, but clearly did not ask for it.[18] On the other hand, how far he could go with the War on Poverty, how many resources we could devote to it, was limited not just by the growing Vietnam War, but also by the lukewarm support for the War on Poverty in the public, even before the riots started in our ghettoes in 1965. What we as a people will push for or, alternatively, simply accept, with or without political leadership, partly depends on our culture.

As we have seen, a central concept of our culture is opportunity, sometimes conceptualized as equality of opportunity. It is more accurate to say we believe in opportunity rather than equality of opportunity because most of us recognize and accept the fact that inevitably some will have more opportunity than others. Perhaps by equality of opportunity we mean some adequate level of opportunity for everyone, for example, through public education. In reality, American citizens think about and understand opportunity in different ways. Some believe that simply by providing public education we are providing opportunity since anyone can "make something of himself." Others believe this is naïve. Even if the latter group has been successful through hard work and the use of their abilities, most do not believe they would have been as successful, maybe not successful at all, had they lived in other circumstances. Part of our political task is to figure out what we should mean by opportunity. Clearly there are connections between what happens to people and their being disadvantaged, which has implications for freedom and the pursuit of happiness we so value. These are matters relevant to the essential purposes of our union. Gaining greater clarity about opportunity and freedom shows we have unfinished work to do in order to be true to our better selves, who we think we are and want to be.

On the Relationship of Markets, Economic Competition, and Self-Love

Most Americans believe in markets and economic competition because of our culture, but more importantly because in our experience we have seen they produce wealth and material well-being. The desire for material well-being relates both to self-love *and* to a desire for the welfare of the public in general. But of course markets, by their very nature, do not give everyone the same outcomes. Outcomes depend on supply, demand, and productivity, among other things. We generally believe the market determines what most people get. We may modify the market and its outcomes some, usually marginally, but we still basically believe in markets. This is related to self-love, the desire to gain things for yourself and your family, but not only to self-love. We also relate markets to freedom, as we understand it, and we value the freedom to seek a good material life for ourselves and our family, not just because of self-love, but because we think freedom is valuable not only for what it allows and produces for us and others, but also because it is valuable in itself. Self-love cannot explain everything we do, but is centrally important.

With our freedom most of us gain what we can materially and then decide what to do with it, usually wanting to use most of what we have gotten for ourselves and our family. In that way also the market is tied to self-love. As we have seen, there is a significant difference between America and most other advanced industrialized democracies, which tax more and spend more with their representative governments making decisions about how the money will be used. These countries, for historical reasons, modify the results of their markets more than we do. These differences continue because their people prefer their way of doing things to ours, possibly because they have had less diverse populations and so they imagine spending money for themselves and people like them rather than for others. This analysis suggests that markets and our valuing of them cannot be explained by self-love alone, yet they serve our self-love and that is one of their purposes.

Notes

1. Alexander Hamilton, James Madison, and John Jay, *The Federalist Papers* (New York: New American Library, 1961), 81.

2. Martha A. Nussbaum, *Upheavals of Thought* (Cambridge: Cambridge University Press, 2001), has done some very good work on compassion.

3. Cotton Mather, *The Ecclesiastical History of New-England* (Hartford, 1820), vol. 1, 116–17.

4. See, for example, the reversal by Congress on catastrophic care coverage in Medicare and on the withholding of taxes on interest from savings accounts.

5. Mancur Olson Jr., *The Logic of Collective Action* (New York: Schocken Books, 1968), 133–34.

6. Olson, *Logic of Collective Action*, 61, sees that moral action can provide selective benefits although he does not emphasize this in his argument.

7. Of course, if people mistake the public bad for the public good, these dynamics can facilitate the creation of public bads. Consequently there is no way to get around the importance of morality, making right choices. To make right choices we need each other and not just those closest to us.

8. Here we should also recognize the importance of the idea of witness, whether it is religiously or secularly based. For one discussion of witness see Hannah Arendt, *Eichmann in Jerusalem* (New York: Penguin Press, 1994), 233, who speaks of Holocaust resisters as important because we can tell their stories and, as a result, the world is a more fit place for human habitation.

9. See the important work of Erwin Hargrove, *The President as Leader* (Lawrence: University Press of Kansas, 1998).

10. Hargrove, *The President*.

11. In 2000 Bill Bradley tried to do this in the Democratic primaries, but his campaign went nowhere.

12. Hargrove, *The President*, 25-48.

13. James MacGregor Burns, *Leadership* (New York: Harper & Row, 1975), 34.

14. Hargrove, *The President*, 49-75.

15. Hargrove, *The President*, 52.

16. Mishnah, Avot 1:14

17. Morality *and* compassion are required since compassion alone can lead to mistaken judgments. See Nussbaum, *Upheavals of Thought*, 414, on the appropriate judgments needed for compassion "allied to a reasonable ethical theory." Nussbaum also recognizes the difficulty of compassion over social barriers, 430. She sees that compassion can but does not necessarily serve morality and that it does not provide a complete guide to it, 390. She argues, correctly in my view, that "it is a guide to something that is at the very heart of morality," 390–91. Nussbaum argues that reasonable judgments about three parts of compassion are needed, judgments about the seriousness of the suffering, whether the suffering person is to blame for his state, and to what extent we should be concerned about the deprivation, 414. Nussbaum also sees that morality without compassion can be formal, empty, and cold. She recognizes that action following compassion may be hard for people to do. To know what is moral of course doesn't necessarily solve that problem because to know the good is not necessarily to do it. That is why many religions say we need God's help in this. Unlike Nussbaum, I have defined compassion as involving action.

18. Robert Dallek, *Flawed Giant: Lyndon Johnson and His Times* (New York: Oxford University Press, 1998), 168–69.

CHAPTER SIX

A Problem of Accountability and Power in Our Democracy

One fundamental idea in our democracy is accountability, that officeholders can and will be held accountable for their actions and inaction. We believe this will influence what they choose to do. An important problem, however, is that sometimes accountability occurs too late, after irretrievable damage has been done. As a possible example, George W. Bush went to war with Iraq as part of the war on terrorism because that made sense to him as good policy. At the time of this writing we do not know the full consequences of that decision, but it is possible that the really bad consequences of that action, if they occur, will come later. For example, if the preventive war with Iraq stimulates additional people to become terrorists, as George W. Tenet, head of the CIA, feared before the war, the action of those terrorists in and on the United States may come later when they are in a position to pull off the kind of major attack they would like to do, probably one involving biological weapons, perhaps chemical and radiological ones, and ultimately nuclear weapons. Most citizens understandably do not want to think about such attacks. They are horrible to contemplate. By the time they occur, if they occur and many governmental officials have warned us they may well occur, in an important sense it will be too late to hold Bush and his policies accountable for at least partly contributing to this development. He may no longer be president and, even if he is, the damage will have been done. To complicate matters even further, no one will be able to say for certain whether those attacks would have occurred had we not attacked Iraq and instead focused on Al Qaeda, but it seems reasonable to suggest that in the intermediate and probably the long run our policy may well increase the likelihood of such attacks as there will be people who want to avenge our action and punish what they see as our arrogance. If these attacks do occur, many could blame Bush's policies for increasing their likelihood, even though his purpose was clearly otherwise, but what good will that do us? There is a serious problem of accountability here, not unique to the Bush presidency but a problem that exists more generally in our democracy and probably in many democracies. Usually in seeking the accountability of officeholders we seek not only to punish them for their actions by not electing them or their party but also to change policy. We can of course do that, but irreparable, catastrophic, and non-rectifiable harm may have occurred. Is there anything we can do to deal with this problem?

One thing we can try to do, whether as officeholders or citizens, is a better job of anticipating the future consequences of our government's actions. We are dealing with an uncertain future so often this is not easy. We can ask that our leaders do a better job anticipating the consequences of their actions, and we must ask our citizens to think more about proposed actions and consequences though many prefer to have problems solved for them, especially in a dangerous world. We also should ask those officeholders critical of our leaders to do a better job of anticipating the future consequences of proposed actions and to speak out. We ask all of this because we love our country and care about its welfare, which is the meaning of patriotism. If we could be confident our leaders would make wise decisions, perhaps we could ask less of ourselves and of those officeholders who are in a position to question likely proposed actions. Too much is at stake in some of these decisions. We cannot just past the buck to our leaders to decide for us.

While it may seem peculiar in a representative democracy to take on such a burden as citizens, it is absolutely in our interest to do so. In the end we select our representatives and leaders, and we simply have to take a more active role in preparing ourselves to be electors and then to monitor their behavior in governing, especially on issues of vital importance, such as decisions that might affect our future safety and security. During the Cold War our citizens generally did not take such an active role, yet we survived and won the Cold War without our taking on such an active role other than supporting our leaders with our treasure and sometimes our blood. But now we are dealing with terrorism in an age of weapons of mass destruction, and we need to accept this new responsibility. The fact that we got through and won the Cold War without playing this sort of role as citizens does not mean we do not need to do it now.

Another way to deal with this problem of accountability, which one could raise serious questions about, is to give less power to the president in foreign policy through a more active use of congressional checks, even though this could pose problems for our role as a superpower and leader in the world and also possibly for our national interest. If Congress more regularly challenged the president, people abroad and at home could ask, who speaks for the United States? Since World War II Congress has generally given control over foreign policy to the White House, and presidents have been aggressive in seeking that control and finding ways to get Congress to accept their leadership. Are we in a new period now where Congress will have to step up to the plate more? In the run up to the war with Iraq of 2003 it was clear that many senators and representatives were reluctant to take Bush on in a strong way over his intentions, most likely because they probably thought we have only one president and to counter him, after he had made his expectations of Iraq and his intentions clear, would have called into question our foreign policy. This would have been seen as particularly problematic after the terrorist attack on America of 9/11. While this was an important consideration, if members of Congress fear disastrous consequences from presidential action or think a proposed action is fundamentally wrong, the patriotic act, the act that shows love of country, is to oppose and criticize that action, not just once but repeatedly since repeated criticism may well be what it takes to move the public. Presidents repeatedly describe what they wish to do and why they propose to do it again and again in an effort to move the public. Opponents need to do the same thing if they are to be heard.

While this is a call for the criticism, checks, and balances that our system is fundamentally based on, since World War II those checks have not been much in evidence in the foreign policy area. Once the president knows he has to share power in this area, he will consult more with Congress before proceeding, and the consultations will be different in a situation of truly shared power and authority and not pro forma as they often are now. Consultation with Congress will involve its congressional leaders, including committee leaders in the foreign policy area. Congress and the president have to find a way to do this besides the president simply informing congressional leaders what he intends to do, usually shortly before he does it. Of course, the more serious terrorist attacks are on the United States, the more likely power, influence, and authority will move toward the president with Congress playing a secondary role.

If we move to a system of shared power in the foreign policy area, there is a possibility that irresponsible partisanship could significantly affect our deliberations, whatever party controls the White House or the Congress. It is not necessarily the case that the greater the danger to America, the less likely it is that such partisanship will occur. That probably partly depends on our perception of the danger. Of course, the stakes involved in decisions on foreign policy and security are great, and we probably have to risk the danger of irresponsible partisanship to get the hoped for benefits of checks and balances in these areas, namely, wiser policy. It is of course true that if the president and Congress do not agree to certain actions, the lack of action could prove to be quite harmful. In the end every one of us has to make a judgment about which arrangements give us greater confidence, given the ever-changing makeup in the White House and Congress and the changing rancor of partisan conflict. While the Constitution stipulates checks and balances and the sharing of power, if Congress doesn't insist on this, it will not happen. The question is whether Congress should insist on this and whether the public should as well. The reason this is such a difficult question is that what the best arrangement of power is in any particular period may depend on who the players are and whether partisanship has escalated to an irresponsible level, which is unpredictable. It is difficult to propose general guidelines about the degree to which power should be shared before one knows the players and the context of partisan hostility. In light of the risks involved, and risks will exist whatever arrangements we decide to support, more serious criticism by the opposition is desirable and would be useful. A real sharing of power is probably desirable for these momentous decisions in foreign policy and security.

Some might argue that in light of Congress's control over the purse and its constitutional authority to declare war, Congress will inevitably share power with the president. However, we have seen wars start without a formal declaration of war by Congress, and we have seen a Congress that was unwilling to challenge the president in the decision to go to war with Iraq after 9/11, even though many representatives and senators had qualms. We have also seen Congress convinced it must continue to appropriate money for our troops, to support those troops in every way needed once they have been committed, and we have seen how hard it was for Congress to be decisive in demanding the end of a war, as in Vietnam. Thus, no formal arrangements will guarantee Congress will have the backbone to stand up to the president in foreign policy just as none will guarantee that Congress or, for that matter, the president will always be wise. The general public has also been reluctant to tell the president ahead of time his policy is misguided, as seen in the decision to go to war with Iraq. If things turn out poorly in Iraq, Congress and the public could react badly as was the case with isolationism in the 1930s in the face of Hitler, an isolationism that resulted from the experience of World War I. With democracy, as with other systems, there are no guarantees all will work out. We simply have to do the best we can.

~

CHAPTER SEVEN

Self-Love and Ignorance about the World as Well as the United States: Can Anything Help Us?

Just as we often ignore the needs of people in this country as we focus on our own needs and wants, we do the same regarding the rest of the world, as do other relatively prosperous people in many countries. The events of 9/11 showed us one result of that. Because of advances in technology and the development of weapons of mass destruction, which inevitably are spreading around the world, we are and will be vulnerable to attack as never before, and it is unlikely we can avoid this vulnerability. Even without weapons of mass destruction, great human, physical, economic, and other costs can be imposed on us because of the disaffection of others. The events of 9/11 showed this. It is very much in our interest and should be the highest priority to figure out what we can do to reduce the motivation of others to do this kind of damage to us, but we seem partly blind to its causes and the distresses of the world as we often are to the distresses of our own country. Self-love, ignorance, and indifference have blinded us in both instances. The evil of others, and it does exist, can provoke a self-righteous as well as a righteous response, and the self-righteousness can reinforce our blindness by making us exclusively focus on the evils of others while ignoring our own flaws. Needless to say, the evil done to us on 9/11 cannot and should not be justified, but our not seeing America's flaws in the world does us no good and is not in our interest.

What will it take for us to get beyond our self-love since doing that may be as essential to our interests as anything we do? There are alternative ways of doing this, which we will briefly examine and assess. We may be able to move beyond excessive self-love because we see it is in our self-interest to do so. This seems almost paradoxical because we are suggesting self-love can be a corrective for blind and excessive self-love, and it can. Unfortunately it is often not clear to us that it is in our self-interest to move beyond excessive self-love. For example, we certainly can continue to use force in response to attacks and potential attacks on us as our major strategy, hoping or assuming this strategy will not catch up with us and will get the job done. We can continue to limit what we do for the have-nots of the world and in response to those who believe our foreign policy is one-sided. We can and probably will take the short-term view and worry about our children and ourselves in the next few years without worrying about what will happen further down the road, including to our grandchildren whose adulthood is not very far away. Eventually, and this could be much sooner than we realize, our actions and approach could catch up with us or our progeny. When those living at the time see what has happened, it may be too late for them to do something about it. Irredeemable damage may have been done. The fact that it is hard to predict the future and that the worst consequences will occur in the future make it less likely we will see what we need to do now. Perhaps we do not care or think much about those yet to come whom we don't know just as we do not care about others that seem far from us, even when they live fairly close and share our time.[1] It is not only parts of our country and the world that are unseen; it is also the future including our future, and that makes it less likely we will do what we need to do. In light of our limitations counting on self-love alone to solve the problems created by self-love probably is a mistake.

Can compassion help us avoid the immoral and quite possibly dire consequences for us of excessive self-love? It seems not, as excessive self-love represents a failure of compassion or its too-limited nature. What will make us compassionate in the way needed, remembering that compassion requires action, not just feeling? The gap between others and ourselves of distance, experience, and time as well as our self-love limit our compassion. Very, very few of us get to experience how the poor in our country or the barely subsisting two-thirds in the world live, and very few of us have a way to know their lives and experience in a way that affects our attitudes and behavior. Perhaps that is one reason why Madison in Federalist No. 10 said we can not count on moral or religious motives to limit our tendency to ignore the rights of others and the aggregate good of the community.[2]

The approach of various religions to this problem is interesting, important, and can be illustrated by a few examples, taken here from Judaism, Christianity, and Islam, but other religions also often focus on compassion and the worst off of us. Basically religion argues that we know or we have been taught what to do and that it is a matter of doing it. Even religions that believe we are sinners assume we know what to do, but simply do not do it. They also believe, if we are redeemed, we will strive to do the good. An example of the view that we know what to do can be seen in Moses's last sermon. "Surely, this Instruction which I enjoin upon you this day is not too baffling for you, nor is it beyond reach. It is not in the heavens, that you should say, 'Who among us can go up to the heavens and get it for us and impart it to us, that we may observe it?' Neither is it beyond the sea, that you should say, 'Who among us can cross to the other side of the sea and get it for us and impart it to us, that we may observe it?' No, the thing is very close to you, in your mouth and in your heart, to observe it."[3] The Ten Commandments tell us what to do and what not to do and, to simplify even further, Rabbi Hillel summarized our obligation while standing on one foot, as he was challenged to do. "What is hateful to you, do not do to your neighbor. This is the entire Torah; the rest is commentary; now go and study."[4] Jesus's Sermon on the Mount tells us what to do. "Therefore, whatever you want men to do to you, do also to them."[5] Islam teaches that no man is a true believer unless he desires for his brother what he wishes for himself.[6] What is interesting is that religions also know often we fail to do what we are supposed to. They can be very realistic. For example, the prophets, Isaiah and Jeremiah, both describe the punishments that will befall the people because they have strayed from God's ways and will be punished by God. The Hebrew Bible is filled with such events. Jesus understands that "narrow is the gate and difficult is the way which leads to life, and there are few who find it."[7] The promise of the Kingdom of Heaven for those who are worthy and Hell for those who deserve it also seems to have a limited effect on people. Yet both the Jewish and Christian religions urge people to change their ways, to be redeemed, which includes changing their actions. Other religions speak to this as well with wisdom and depth. Nonetheless, religious teaching seems not to be enough as we continue to ignore it or only follow it sometimes.

Some people, Kant is an example, turned to morality to deal with the problem we have focused on. So did Rousseau, Rawls, and numerous other philosophers. But how has that affected practice? Obviously no better than religion as a solution to this dilemma.

Given limits in the achievements of all these approaches to dealing with the problem of self-love, what shall we do? *What are needed are the multiple fronts of self-love, compassion, religion, and morality* with none of them either separately or together providing a panacea or a guarantee we can solve this problem, but they provide our best chance. This is a problem faced by every generation, a human problem. Individually and collectively we have the capacity to choose how we shall live, what we shall care about and what we shall do. Our task is to make good choices. We should use and benefit from whatever can help us do this. Most people want to live morally better lives than they are living and want to make their country and the world better places. Compassion, morality, and religion provide ways to live such lives if only we will use them and pay loving attention to them as many of us pay attention to our children, our gardens, or whatever else we love and care about. Paradoxically, compassion, morality, and religion not only could help us live better lives, but also would serve our self-interest, if only we could see that. Once we see the importance of these multiple fronts of compassion, morality, and religion, it becomes clear they are a proper and important part of the study of politics because of their great effect on it and their centrality in it.[8]

Is less selfishness on our part realistic, that is, can we and will we do it? We can because what is required is a balancing, of being for ourselves and being for others and not just members of our family, group, community, and country, valuable as these are. The question of course is what kind of balance we will do. Will people balance their self-love enough? To do so requires morality, compassion, and religion, a morality and religion that involve loving and helping others, not harming them.[9]

What Is to Be Done

What can we do to move our country toward a better balance between self-love and the love of others? Our first task is to recognize our excessive or unbalanced self-love, but then what? Changing our motives and purposes is critical as is honesty about what we are and are not doing and its consequences. Clearly we citizens need to be better informed, and a media that can better present government, politics, and policy and do so in an interesting way is needed. We also need to care about the outcomes of others, which may well be the most important and most difficult challenge we face. Certain other changes in our political system would also help. The public financing of congressional and other elections combined with limits on private financing would help as that could affect who seeks office and what they do, once in office.

How can we, using our political system, act individually and collectively, to create a better balance between our self-love and our love of others? Some people are already doing this. They are active politically in various ways. We also have to be willing to devote more of our private resources to others in and outside of our country. We have to support leaders who take the initiative in this effort, which they will if they believe we will support them. We also need to recognize a significant role for government since private charity alone, while important, cannot get the job done. Where part of the business community can find a way to benefit economically from bettering our world, as they can with environmental, energy, and other initiatives, it will play a part. *We as citizens must also believe our actions including our civic actions will make a difference, as we often believe our actions in the private sector will when we serve our more self-loving purposes.* Most of us are committed to our families. We must extend that commitment. When results are slow in coming, if people believe their actions are worth doing, in themselves and in what they produce, they are more likely to keep at it.

One useful thing some citizens can do is go into public service. Reducing the role of money in politics will encourage more good people to do this. To redress the balance between self-love and love of others requires efforts by organized and mobilized people, elite action, support of the people, and on some occasions mass action. The methods people will use and the actions they take will resemble many of the actions we now see in our political system, but the purposes of those actions will differ from our current purposes as will their consequences. We will serve others as well as ourselves. This is demanding, but it is what we were meant for.

What Happens if We Cannot Deal with the Problems Caused by Excessive Self-Love?

If we are unable to deal with the problems caused by excessive self-love, what are and will be the consequences? Excessive self-love is not a new problem; it is as old as recorded history. It has produced bitter fruits, suffering, and destruction as well as positive achievements. But there are new realities in our time, potentially devastating realities, and what we do in the immediate future may affect whether and to what extent *we* suffer the consequences of our excessive self-love. What are the foreseeable and possible consequences?

One consequence will be a continuation of what we see already, an unacceptable *and unsustainable* degree of inequality of opportunity in our country and the world and a denial of basic necessities and rights to people in our country and the world. It is likely the inequality will increase. If no other consequence occurred, this would be bad enough and should be a source of embarrassment and even shame. But more is at stake than this. The world is changing, and it is unlikely we can go on as we have been. The development of technology and the inevitable spread of weapons of mass destruction mean that sooner or later terrorists are likely to get these weapons and use them against the more prosperous and powerful parts of the world, most likely with a special focus on the United States as the most powerful and rich country in the world. While we can fight a war against terrorism, it is unlikely we can stop all the terrorist attacks against us. It is also likely our war on terrorism will create new cadres of terrorists out for revenge who want to show us they cannot be controlled by us and can do us great harm. What we can and must do is seek to change the circumstances that produce terrorists and that includes reducing inequalities in the world. The goal, of course, is not to eliminate inequality for that is not likely to happen and is not desirable, but rather to help people gain the basic necessities of life, including increasing their opportunity to gain these through productive labor, and also supporting their efforts to control their own political lives. People want to believe that they and their children are moving in the right direction materially, that things will be better for their children. That is our opening because we can help them do this. Those who do not want us to be successful will of course try to disrupt our efforts. In addition, we will have to deal with the problems of corruption, the wasting of what we contribute, and the task of making sure our assistance affects those at the bottom, not just the top 20 percent. Nevertheless, these obstacles are not greater than others we have successfully overcome.

It is absolutely in our moral and material interest to deal with the problems caused by excessive self-love. If we do not, our futures will be bleak. Of course, excessive self-love is not our only problem. We must also deal with our arrogance, our self-righteousness, and our desire to control what happens in the world in ways that cause great and widespread alienation and reaction. We also need to recognize that our helping the less well off do better and our infringing on them less culturally so they are free to become who they wish to be will not entirely solve the problem of those who wish to do us evil, which is why there will always be a role for force, even as our principal thrust should be generosity. We cannot entirely control the world, but we can help make it a more hospitable place for ourselves and others.

There is even a more fundamental reason why we should deal with the excesses of our self-love. That is our job, our task here on Earth, not just for what it produces in the lives of others but also for what it means in our own lives. By dealing with excessive self-love, we will change who we are and we will be more worthy of the love of our Creator, others, and ourselves. The most profound reasons to deal with the excesses of self-love are religious and philosophical. We are given choices in life, some of us have fewer constraints and more opportunities, some of us more constraints and fewer opportunities, but we all have choices in how we live, how we are with others and ourselves.

Our task in life is to figure out what we are supposed to do and then do it, in practical and effective ways. This is a lifetime task, one worthy of us and of the blessings of life we have received.

Notes

1. Alexis de Tocqueville, *Democracy in America*, trans. Harvey C. Mansfield and Delba Winthrop, Harvey C. Mansfield and Delba Winthrop eds. (Chicago: University of Chicago Press, 2000), 482–84.

2. Alexander Hamilton, James Madison, and John Jay, *The Federalist Papers* (New York: New American Library, 1961), 81.

3. Deuteronomy 30:11–14.

4. Babylonian Talmud, Shabbat 31a.

5. Matthew 7:2.

6. This is a Hadith, which are the sayings of Mohammed. It is not in the Koran.

7. Matthew 7:14.

8. Since the arts including literature can affect compassion and morality, they are also a proper and important part of the study of politics.

9. My own view is that we participate in creation through our choices, which contribute to creating the world we live in, and that it was intended that we do so.

~

That We Can Change: A Short Appendix on Love of Self and Others

When my concern for others changes, who I am changes. I change and what loving myself means changes. I am acting in accord with a changed I. My self-interest also changes and how I conceive it changes. This reduces the tension between love of self and love of others. To love myself, to be who I am, includes loving others, caring about them and what happens to them. Similarly, once I can put myself in others' shoes, what loving my neighbor as myself means changes. All this is very important because it suggests the way in which we can change once we care about others, not just those in our family. This does not tell us how to cause this change or what leads people to or away from this love, subjects of great and continuing importance, but it shows the way in which we can change to reduce the tension between love of self and love of others.

Practically all of us have heard the injunction, "Love thy neighbor as thyself," but note what that means. First you have to love yourself, but what does that mean? One of its meanings is you forgive yourself for your weaknesses and shortcomings, even as you try to change them, just as you forgive others for theirs. As the Lord's Prayer says, "Forgive our debts as we forgive our debtors." We of course change when we do this. These sorts of changes are enormously important and merit our attention and study.

Bibliography

Arendt, Hannah. *Eichmann in Jerusalem*. New York: Penguin, 1994.

Armstrong, Karen. *Buddha*. New York: Penguin, 2001.

———. *The Spiral Staircase*. New York: Knopf, 2004.

Arnold, R. Douglas. *The Logic of Congressional Action*. New Haven, CT: Yale University Press, 1990.

Babylonian Talmud. Edited and translated by Isidore Epstein. London: Soncino Press, 1961.

Bible. *Holy Bible*. Nashville: Thomas Nelson Publishers, 1990.

Birnbaum, Jeffrey H., and Alan S. Murray. *Showdown at Gucci Gulch: Lawmakers, Lobbyists, and the Unlikely Triumph of Tax Reform*. New York: Vintage, 1987.

Blumenauer, Earl, and Jim Leach. "Redistricting, a Bipartisan Sport." *New York Times*, 8 July 2003, A23.

Burns, James MacGregor. *Leadership*. New York: Harper & Row, 1975.

———. *The Lion and the Fox*. New York: Harcourt, Brace, 1957.

Dallek, Robert. *Flawed Giant: Lyndon Johnson and His Times*. New York: Oxford University Press, 1998.

Donald, David Herbert. *Lincoln*. New York: Simon & Schuster, 1995.

Fenno, Richard F., Jr. *Home Style: House Members in Their Districts*. Boston: Little, Brown, 1978.

Fitzpatrick, John C., ed. *Writings of George Washington*. New York: Greenwood Press, 1970.

Fromm, Erich. *Escape from Freedom*. New York: Avon Books, 1941.

Goldin, Judah. *The Living Talmud*. New York: New American Library, 1957.

Goodwin, Doris Kearns. *Lyndon Johnson and the American Dream*. New York: St. Martin's Griffin, 1976.

Hamilton, Alexander, James Madison, and John Jay. *The Federalist Papers*. New York: New American Library, 1961.

Hargrove, Erwin C. *The President as Leader*. Lawrence: University Press of Kansas, 1998.

Hartz, Louis. *The Liberal Tradition in America*. New York: Harcourt, Brace, 1955.

Jacobson, Gary C. *The Politics of Congressional Elections*. Fifth Edition. New York: Longman, 2001.

Johnson, Haynes, and David S. Broder. *The System*. Boston: Little, Brown, 1996.

Kozol, Jonathan. *The Shame of the Nation*. New York: Crown Publishers, 2005.

Mather, Cotton. *The Ecclesiastical History of New-England* (Hartford, 1820).

Mayhew, David R. *Congress: The Electoral Connection*. New Haven, CT: Yale University Press, 1974.

McPherson, James M. *Battle Cry of Freedom*. New York: Random House, 1988.

Neustadt, Richard E. *Presidential Power and Modern Presidents*. New York: Free Press, 1990.

Nussbaum, Martha A. *Upheavals of Thought:The Intelligence of Emotions*. Cambridge: Cambridge University Press, 2001.

Olson, Mancur, Jr. *The Logic of Collective Action*. New York: Schocken Books, 1968.

Putnam, Robert D. *Making Democracy Work*. Princeton, NJ: Princeton University Press, 1993.

Schattschneider, E. E. *The Semisovereign People*. New York: Holt, Rinehart, and Winston, 1960.

The Mishnah. Translated by Jacob David Herzog. New York: Bloch, 1947.

Tocqueville, Alexis De. *Democracy in America*. Translated and edited by Harvey C. Mansfield and Delba Winthrop. Chicago: University of Chicago Press, 2000.

Victoria Newfeldt, ed. *Webster's New World College Dictionary*. New York: Macmillan, 1997.

Waldman, Sidney. "How Congress Does the Difficult." *PS: Political Science and Politics* XXXIII, no. 4 (2000): 803–808.

Weaver, R. Kent. *Automatic Government*. Washington, DC: The Brookings Institution, 1988.

Wills, Gary. *Lincoln at Gettysburg*. New York: Simon & Schuster, 1992.

Woodward, Bob. *The Agenda*. New York: Simon & Schuster, 1994.

Index

119

~

About the Author

Sidney R. Waldman is Professor of Political Science at Haverford College. He specializes in American politics, particularly Congress, the presidency, and public policy analysis. His previous books include *The Foundations of Political Action: An Exchange Theory of Politics* and *Congress and Democracy*, coauthored with David Vogler.